Bundle Book

Real Estate Investing:

How To Make Your Riches From Rental Properties and Flipping Houses, And Build Passive Income By Mastering The Property Investment Game

By Brandon Anderson

Table of Contents

Introduction

Congratulations on downloading *Real Estate Investing: How To Make Your Riches From Rental Properties and Flipping Houses, And Build Passive Income By Mastering The Property Investment Game* and thank you for doing so. Regardless if you are looking to start investing for the first time or are looking to enhance an existing investment portfolio, real estate is an ideal choice. Ideal, that is, if you choose wisely, but the complex ins and outs of the various types of real estate investment make doing so far from a sure thing.

To help make the process more straight forward, the following chapters will discuss everything you need to know in order to get started with real estate investment successfully starting with the basics including useful investment lingo, how to decide if real estate if real estate is right for you and additional starter tips to help you get started on the right foot. Next, you will learn essentials when it comes to paying for property, finding the ideal property and negotiating the deal when the time comes.

From there you will learn about a wide variety of different real estate investment opportunities including rental property of the traditional and turn key variety as well as the responsibilities that come with being a landlord. You will then learn the ins and out of property flipping including determining when a property is a good deal and building a fix and flip team. Finally, you will learn the basics of property wholesaling and REITs as well.

There are plenty of books on this subject on the market, thanks again for choosing this one! Every effort was made to ensure it is full of as much useful information as possible, please enjoy!

Chapter 1: Why Real Estate?

Real estate is one of the most time-honored investment strategies because, baring the occasional recession, housing prices are almost always going to slowly but surely rise as land is one of the few things that they aren't currently making more of. Investing in real estate means taking on benefits associated with net worth, profitability, cash flow, liquidity, and diversification. Another reason that real estate is the ideal investment choice for the burgeoning investor is that there are so many different real estate investment options to choose from. It doesn't matter what amount you are looking to invest, or what time frame you are hoping to profit in, real estate investment is a viable solution for you.

When it comes to investing in real estate, potential investors have a wide variety of options depending on how hands on they wish to be with their investment. What's more, all types of real estate investment are virtually guaranteed to make at least the industry average 7 percent return on their investment, assuming the market doesn't take one of its infrequent nose dives in the interim. Passive real estate investment can take the form of rental properties that are managed via a property management service, real estate investment trusts which are essential stocks for real estate investment or wholesaling property.

Rental properties are always an attractive option because you know that the property is increasing in value in the long term, while you still make a profit in the short term. Plus, there is nothing like owning an investment that you can physically touch, see and feel. REITs were designed to allow those with relatively limited financial resources to take advantage of the ownership of larger properties including things like shopping centers, office buildings, and hotels. Investors buy into specific REITs and receive a return on their investment equal to the size of the share that they own. Finally, wholesaling property is similar to flipping a property, except without any of the renovation work. In this investment scenario you find a property that has potential, arrange to buy it for a profitable price and then sell that contract to someone who actually follows through on the work, plus several thousand dollars for your time.

Regardless of what type of real estate investment you fancy, you will find that you can make money in four different ways. The first is through a process known as appreciation which is the name given to the natural increase in the value of a given property over time. While this typically amounts to less than 5 percent per year, it is a constant that you don't need to work to generate which means it is, in essence, free money. While appreciation is nice, it is important to never go about making real estate investments based solely on what you believe the appreciation of a property to be, there are always going to be more profitable reasons to consider and if there isn't then the property is a poor value anyway.

Rather than placing an abundance of value on appreciation alone, the best way to go about accurately determining the value of a potential property is to consider the various ways you could make money from it. Investing in property doesn't have to just be places like condominiums or houses, they could also be storage units, laundry mats, car washes and even major investments like large office buildings or hotels. Depending on the type of investment you choose, you may also be able to count on secondary profit streams thanks to pay to use items like vending machines.

Talk the talk

When it comes to being taken seriously in the real estate community and related fields it is important that you understand the jargon and lingo you are likely to encounter on the regular. While you will always want to ask someone to explain a term you haven't heard before as opposed to blindly pressing forward, showing the other person that you know your stuff is still the best-case scenario.

Adverse use: If someone is using a property without the property owner's permission then that property is said to be in the midst of adverse use.

Agreement of sale: The agreement of sale is a document created by a buyer who is interested in purchasing a property that includes the terms they are proposing and any agreement that needs to be outlined between buyer and seller.

Amortization: When the price of a given property is listed as the price that will need to be paid each month that price is said to amortize.

Back to back escrow: Back to back escrow is a situation that occurs when an investor finds themselves working to close a deal on one property while at the same time selling their own property as part of a separate transaction.

Balloon payment: If the payment for a given property is split into multiple payments and the final payment is greater than the average for the other payments then it is referred to as a balloon payment.

Capital gains tax: This is a federal tax that you are required to pay each year based on the appreciation of each property that you own.

Cap rate: Cap rate is the total amount of all profits made from a particular investment property over a specific period of time.

Days on the market: This is the number of the days that a property was listed for sale before it was sold.

Examination of title: When a property is going to be sold, the title that guarantees ownership of it is officially inquired upon and the examination of title results in a list of all of the previous owners going all the way back to when the property was built.

Equity: This is the term given to the total amount the owner of the property can expect to make off of it once all of the relevant expenses accrued in selling it has been taken into account.

Forbearance: Forbearance occurs when a property is in the early stages of foreclosure and the loan lender agrees to put the process on hold and also forgives any late payments the owner of the property currently owes.

Notice of Default: If you own a property and purchased it with a loan, that you are currently not making agreed upon payments on then you will receive a notice of default which lets you know the lender is taking steps to put the property into a state of foreclosure.

Title insurance: This form of insurance protects either the buyer or the seller of a particular piece of property in case the property itself ends up in the middle of a legal dispute.

Walkthrough: This is the final time when the future owner of a property visits the property to make sure everything is on the level before signing the final contract and taking ownership of it.

Is real estate investment right for you?

While real estate is a viable choice for a vast majority of investors, that doesn't mean that it is going to be right for everyone, right now. There are several things you should consider before making the leap as, regardless of the type of real estate investment you choose, it can be a complicated and lengthy endeavor. It is important to take a realistic look at your current situation, and ask yourself the following questions before you make any concrete investing plans.

What are your short term and long term objectives?
When creating a plan, you are going to want to start by determining objectives for your investing, which can be broken down into three primary categories, growth, income and safety. If your objective is safety, then you are going to want to focus on keeping the wealth you already have above all else which means that only the bare minimum of risk is allowed. If you are hoping to create a constant stream of income then your objective is going to, unsurprisingly, be income. Finally, if your objective is growth then you are interested in the prospects of the long-term rather than any individual gains that are often based around capital appreciation. When choosing your objectives, you are going to want to be realistic and always factor in your ideal level of risk.

What is your level of risk tolerance?
While every investor's goal is going to be to ultimately end up with more wealth than they started with, the details regarding the specifics are primarily determined by the overall amount of risk that they can tolerate. To understand the concept of risk as it relates to investing, it is important to keep in mind that the various markets that relate to the types of investments in the following chapter are all known to be volatile to one degree or another. The level of volatility a market is prone to is related to the overall amount of movement that the market is going to feel in a given period of time. Investments that are highly volatile are likely to pay out better than those that have a lower volatility, but the chance that you will lose your initial investment is going to be greater as well. Remember, there is no one right way to invest, high volatility or low is primarily a personal preference.

Are you ready to start investing in the long-term?
Current estimates put the amount needed to retire successfully at greater than $500,000. Despite this fact, a vast majority of individuals are not currently saving anywhere near enough to allow them to support themselves throughout their twilight years. If you are at a point in your life where you are stable enough to consider investing successfully, it may help to first consider what your current income is compared to your monthly bills.

What is your support system like?
While having a support system is always recommended when it comes to making the wisest investments possible, it is especially crucial when you are first getting into real estate investment as there are so many different variables that need to be accounted for in order for the investment to turn out the way you are anticipating. Knowing that you have someone available to run potential deals by can make it easier to invest with confidence so you don't have to worry about secretly losing your shirt with your first deal.

Real estate investment is much more complex than simply purchasing properties and then selling them for a profit which means you will benefit greatly from the insight that a local real estate investment club could provide. These clubs are available in most reasonably sized cities or, barring that, an online forum with an active community could help in much the same way.

Starter Tips

Start an LLC: If you are thinking about investing in real estate, one of the first things that you are going to want to do is to look into the specifics of setting up a Limited Liability Corporation to be in charge of any investments that you make. Doing so will ensure that your personal assets are secure in case something goes wrong down the line somewhere and an accident occurs that is outside the realm that your insurance can pay for. Alternately, if the investment doesn't work out and you are left with debt related to the endeavor, you can simply shutter the LLC and walk away. An LLC can be set up online for as little as $200. While this might seem like an unnecessary step when it comes to real estate investment you are always going to want to try your hardest to plan for the worst while still hoping for the best. Go ahead and take the time to set up your LLC now, if the time comes where you need it, you will be glad you did.

Consider an IRA: IRA is short for Individual Retirement Account and it is a savings account that anyone can set up that offers big tax breaks in return for a strict lock on the funds until you reach retirement age. Much like a 401(k), an IRA lets you invest the money you put into it in a wide variety of ways, including securities and even real estate. There is a limit to how much you can add to them, however, as those under the age of fifty are currently limited to $5,500 per year. Those over fifty are limited to $6,500 per year. You are then allowed to write off your contributions on your taxes.

The limits on IRA investments are pretty broad, you aren't allowed to use it as loan collateral, buy real estate for personal use or lend it to yourself but otherwise, the sky's the limit. While the money you earn on your IRA will be taxed as regular income when you withdrawal it, if you invest in a Roth IRA instead, then your money can grow tax-free. Roth IRAs are funded with post-tax dollars so you will have already paid the required taxes on the funds. Additionally, you are free to leave your money in a Roth IRA for as long as you like, unlike a traditional IRA which requires you to start withdrawing the funds once you hit 59.5 years of age.

Chapter 2: Paying for It

If you are interested in purchasing property as a form of passive income for the smallest amount down possible, you are going to need to put in an extreme amount of time, have a fantastic credit score, be very lucky or some combination of the three. Even then, amazing real estate deals are most certainly the exception, not the rule, and a majority of the properties on the market at any given time are going to require a decent down payment in order to close the deal. With that being said, as long as you are smart about how you make your initial investment you are virtually guaranteed to make a reliable return in the long run.

Consider your circumstances: It is important to consider how stable your career is as a whole, not just your current job. If you are in a risky industry then you need to consider if you feel secure enough in your finances, and the city that you live in, to know that you aren't going to want to move the moment that your current opportunity wraps up. It is important to be honest with yourself during this analysis and to really be sure in your choice as buying a home and then selling it within just a few years is likely going to cost you money, rather than being a profitable investment.

While it's true that you can likely afford to purchase a property for about what you are currently paying in rent, the truth of the matter is that owning a property is about more than that financially. Owning a property means paying homeowner's insurance, HOA fees (if applicable), property taxes and more. Additionally, you can expect your utilities to increase as you will now be on the hook for garbage collection, water, and sewer expenses that you were quite possibly not paying as a renter. What's more, before you go ahead and pull the trigger you are going to want to have a separate fund set aside to pay for in-the-moment home repairs if you don't want to risk dipping into your emergency fund as you know it will come in handy eventually.

Speaking of costs, while in certain circumstances you will be able to qualify for a home mortgage loan through the Federal Housing Administration which means you could get a home for as little as 3.5 percent of the total cost; the majority of home loans that you come across won't be so generous. If you plan on going to a traditional bank for a loan, then you will need to ensure that your credit score is greater than 700 and that your debt coverage ratio is currently greater than 1.25.

Borrowing from a position of strength

In order to ensure you get the best deal on your loan as possible, it is important to know what tools you have at your disposal when it comes to finding the right type of financing. To get started, you are going to want to check your credit report and seek professional help if your score isn't where you want it to be. Unfortunately, a high credit score isn't all that is required these days as the Great Recession has made it much more difficult to finance an investment property than it once was. This means you will naturally start at a disadvantage if you don't have an extensive credit history or lots of previous investment experience. Difficult is a long way from impossible, however, as long as you approach lenders with the following:

Significant down payment: Currently most traditional lenders are going to require that you have at least 20 percent of the total cost of the investment you are requesting financing for in hand before they will give the go ahead. If you are considering hard money lenders (discussed in detail later in this chapter) then you will likely need 40 percent instead. However, if you can put down an extra 5 percent then you will likely start to see a significant decrease in rates almost immediately. Being able to offer up a larger down payment will also make it more likely that financial institutions will be more forgiving when it comes to overlooking less than perfect credit; this will only take you so far, however.

If you don't have the full 20 percent down payment for the property you are considering, but you qualify for a bank loan in all other respects, then you may want to consider getting two loans rather than just one, just keep in mind that it is going to cut into your profits substantially and it can be more difficult than getting just one mortgage as well. If you do go down this path it is important to plan to pay off one of the mortgages as quickly as possible in order to reduce the overall amount of interest that you ultimately pay.

When approaching a lender, you will want to do so with a well thought out and researched plan that shows a high value to loan ratio as well as a credit score of 740 or higher if you hope to score the best interest rates. If your credit score is lower, the only way you can expect the same rate is by paying more or by paying the same amount and taking a higher interest rate. Regardless, you will want to be able to show that you have the ability to pay all of your expenses for a full six months, plus the expenses of the new property as well if you hope to be considered acceptable.

As a new real estate investor you will likely find that you have better luck trying local banks, as they will already have a legitimate interest in keeping the local economy humming along. They are also likely to have more flexible options more especially tailored for investors in your situation as are mortgage brokers who may also be willing to finance your real estate investment dreams. You won't want to take the first rate they offer you, however, as like in all things related to real estate investment you will find much greater success, and savings, when you do your research. If you are working with a local real estate investment club, which is strongly recommended, they would be the place to start when it comes to the best local lender recommendations.

Finding a lender
If you plan on purchasing not just a single investment rental property but many, then you will likely want to take the extra time to make the effort to find a lender with whom you can build a mutually beneficial long term relationship with. This type of relationship will, in turn, make it easier for the pair of you to come up with a strategy that ensures everyone comes out a winner, not just on this first interaction but during every subsequently one thereafter. You will want to be wary of real estate brokers, however, as they are not going to offer you the freedom to purchase the ugly duckling properties of your dreams. Remember, the lender is going to directly be responsible for distributing your loans which means it is important to interview them before you full commit to anything. Questions you should ask include things like:

- What is the total number of investors that you are currently working with?
- How many loans would I be able to have active at a single time??
- What types of real estate investments to do you favor?

These questions and other like them will make it easier for you to choose a lender with confidence based on facts, not sales pitches. Remember, if you don't like something about an individual that's completely fine, as long as you act accordingly and move on to keep from wasting everyone's time in both the short and the long run. If you can't seem to find the lender that's right for you, it is important to not despair and to instead keep at it. If you are looking to put down as little up front as you possibly can, title loans, credit cards or equity loans based on other property that you own are always an option, though they should be exercised with caution.

Lender alternatives

P2P: Over the past few years a number of peer-to-peer (P2P) real estate investment websites have popped up offering both short term and long term loan options for those interested in buying and fixing up a property without the cash on hand to pay for it themselves.

Investing in these types of loans is often referred to as Trust Deed investing which means the investor is a private source of capital which is then loaned to the borrower. This investment is secured by a Trust Deed, hence the name and is the same regardless of which P2P lending platform you decide to use.

P2P real estate loans often have a number of benefits when it compared with more traditional bank loans, the first of which is that they are much easier for those seeking loans to qualify for. They are also often much less rigid in terms of guidelines than traditional loans and often go through in a matter of hours, not weeks or months. They are also ideal for those looking to generate passive income streams because they don't require the investment of the full price of the property as with real world transactions. Instead, investors are able to invest the amount they are comfortable with and a clear idea of the repayment terms they can expect.

As with any other type of real estate investment, it is important to have a clear idea of the risks and benefits associated with the property in question. To that end, it is important to have a basic understanding of what the After Repair Value (ARV) of any property you are looking at is going to be. ARV can be thought of as the amount the property is going to be worth once the project is fully finished. This amount needs to be enough to cover the proposed costs of purchasing the property as well as renovations with enough left over to turn a profit for the person who is working on the property.

Owner financing: Depending on how you plan on making a profit from the property, you may find that asking the seller for owner financing can be a reliable way to ensure that you don't need to worry about a loan at all, as long as you can get rid of the property before the inspection window closes and you actually need to come up with the money. Prior to 2009, practically anyone could get an investment property loan as long as they were able to actually walk into a bank and ask about receiving one. As such, those who couldn't a loan via traditional means was naturally mistrusted which meant asking about owner financing was a no go.

Things are different these days, however, as it is public knowledge that banks are more skittish when it comes to giving out loans and sellers are more willing to just get things done regardless of how the deal gets made. In fact, currently, more than 30 percent of all sellers are willing to consider owner financing for the right buyer which means you are going to need to have everything prepared from the previous chapter in order to show that you are a reliable investment. Once you do obtain owner financing you will then sign a promissory note saying when you will pay back the loan in full, what your monthly payments are going to be, when these payments start and what the interest rate is like.

If you have access to a contractor who can get materials on credit, then it is possible that you could sell the owners on the idea of selling you the house with the promise to pay them in full once it is renovated and resold for more than it is going for now. This will obviously not be feasible in all situations, but for owners who are already fairly well off who are not selling for emergency reasons this can be thought of as a type of investment and if you can prove them numbers you might be on to something.

Chapter 3: Finding Property Basics

It doesn't matter what type of real estate investment you are looking forward to investing in, you won't be able to realistically move forward if you aren't able to find a property that will end up putting enough money in your pocket to be worth all the hard work. Luckily, you won't be without options when it comes to finding the best properties for the cheapest possible price.

Find the right area
In order to be successful when you look for properties to purchase it is vital that you take the time to research your target areas ahead of time to prevent yourself from wasting time looking at details of properties that aren't going to work out in the long-term and also to ensure that when you find a good deal you are aware of what you have on your hands and can plan accordingly. Finally, this research is important when it comes to knowing if the price a seller is asking for is reasonable or completely off base.

In order to find the right area to focus on you are going to want to choose one that has properties of varying price ranges and a property tax rate that is low for the area. Checking into the property tax rate is a crucial step in the process because properties that are only a few streets from one another could have wildly different tax rates.

It is important to visit any areas you are considering in person and talk to the locals to make sure there isn't anything hiding just under the surface that you are missing. You can learn more about most neighborhoods by spending 15 minutes in them in person than you can reading about them for an hour or more online. You will want to get a feel for the neighborhood and its charms as well as the people who call it home. The best people to talk to are often renters as those who own a property in an area are more likely to make excuses for it. You should also check with the local police station for current crime statistics.
You will also want to consider the main attractions around the neighborhoods that you are considering and how they would appeal to your primary renting audience. Are you looking for someplace a family might want to call home? Then check out the schools in the area and make finding property near the best ones a priority. On the contrary, maybe the nightlife potential is more of a factor, whatever it is, doing your homework means more than simply knowing everything there is to know about the home in question.

Regardless of your target audience, it is always beneficial to look at properties that are close to a local business district and also to always keep abreast of any major changes coming to the area such as companies moving into or out of town. If a big company is coming in then they are likely going to be bringing new employees with them while if the company is on its way out then you know to avoid the area in case it can't recover from the loss.

Finding Properties through Online Listings
The most basic and freest option that you have when you're looking for a good real estate to purchase is no longer a newspaper. Instead, it's the internet. In addition to Zillow and the MLS database, some other sites that will be able to provide you with quality online listings include the following:

LoopNet.com: Unlike Zillow, LoopNet is able to provide its users with exclusively commercial real estate opportunities. To this end, there are advantages to using LoopNet that you won't find elsewhere. These include being able to compare sale prices within a given locale, as well as look at a property's history as well as provide you with information regarding purchase and selling trends.

Auction.com: If you're looking for a property that you could possibly acquire for cheaper than its market value and you have a knack for the foreclosure or short sale market, then using Auction.com should be a no-brainer. With Auction.com, you don't have to travel to a physical location in order to partake in the auction process if you don't want to. You're able to participate in auctions online, as well as be offered the ability to travel to locations where an auction is taking place. This site also keeps track of auctions in various parts of the nation and updates this information on their website in the form of a calendar.

Craigslist: Craigslist? Really? While Craigslist might get a bad rep, the reality is that it can be a great place to find homes that are being sold by owners and people who do not desire to work with a Realtors. Craigslist can also be a great starting point for when you're looking to negotiate with people and get them to lower their prices. This is especially true if they're not working with a Realtors, or they feel as if their property is too rundown to be considered profitable by a real estate agent.

MLS

The multiple listing service (MLS) is an excellent place to look for current listings as it contains a regularly updated list of all of the properties on the market in the country that are being sold by licensed realtors. As anyone is free to look at the current list, you can expect the best deals to go quite quickly which means if you are going to go this route you are going to want to check it around 5 am EST and again before you go to bed in order to ensure you don't miss out on the best deals.

Even with this level of diligence, you should still be prepared for some stiff competition, however, as there are as many great deals on the site as there are people who are looking to take advantage of them. Generally speaking, you can plan on finding the best deals first thing Monday and Friday morning as these will be the days that include the least competition. This is because working in real estate allows for an extremely flexible schedule which many people use as an excuse to take a weekend that starts early or ends late. Thus, if you make the extra effort on these days you can reap the rewards.

Know what you are looking for: When looking through the MLS listings, the most important thing to keep an eye out for are properties that have been on the market once and are now back for a repeat performance. What this means is that the original deal for the property fell through which also means the owner is far more likely to be willing to negotiate than would otherwise be the case. These types of sellers are often just looking to be done with the entire process which means you can often find a great deal if you are the first person to show up with cash in hand or preapproved for a loan.

Finally, MLS is useful because sometimes you will simply get lucky. There are thousands of new MLS listings every day which means if you keep it up you are virtually guaranteed to stumble across a good deal eventually. Sometimes it might be in the form of a short sale that you see just as it is listed or you might find a property that is listed low expressly to be sold quickly. This is why it is worth checking each and every day, you never know what might be waiting on the next page.

Sellers who are motivated

If you are really looking to pick up properties on the cheap, then you may want to avoid MLS completely by looking for properties that have not yet made it to that part of the process. This means looking for sellers who you have reason to believe are especially motivated and doing something that benefits both parties. The goal is to find sellers who have yet to reach out to a real estate agent, leaving you far more in control than may otherwise be the case. Once a seller goes ahead and hires a real estate agent the possibility of getting the best possible deal goes out the window which is why reaching out to those who have not yet thought about selling their home such an effective tactic.

Where to find them: The first thing you need in order for this process to be successful is, unsurprisingly, to find the type of homeowners who would be classified as motivated sellers which are people who are currently in urgent need of a serious influx of cash for to the point that their debts are already in collections and the fact that someone might come and take their home may have already occurred to them. The easiest way to find a list of people in this situation is to go online and find a company that will sell you a list of debtors in your area. This should only take a few minutes in even a small city and will likely set you back between $200 and $300.

After you have this list the next step is to head to the local clerk of the court to cross check the names you have with a list of property owners to see who on your list warrants a closer look. Once you have finished narrowing down your list, the next thing you will want to do is generate a form letter to mail to your motivated sellers. The basics of your letter should include lip service towards their plight as well as a concise explanation of how you can help them and the fact that you have access to enough money to clear their debt completely. You will want to stop short of making an offer at the moment, however, as this is better done in person where you can get a clear measure of the state the motivated seller is in. You will finish the letter with your contact details and then let the deals come to you.

While not every person you send a letter to will contact you, it will only take a small number of interested parties to keep you busy for a year or more. Generally speaking, you can expect a direct mailing campaign targeted in this way to see a roughly 3 percent response which means that for every 100 letters you send out 3 people will be in touch. Thus, for a minimal monetary and time investment, you can virtually guarantee a steady supply of sellers who are interested in talking to you without having to deal with competition in any shape or form. What's more, the properties you purchase in this way are virtually guaranteed to be available for less than market value.

Courthouse auction: While not available everywhere, in many states, you will find that if a lean holder forecloses on a property the last step is for the property to be auctioned off. While these types of auctions rarely take place at the actual courthouse these days, they remain an excellent way to purchase property for pennies on the dollar, though the amount of information you have on the property in question is going to vary dramatically. Details for these types of auctions can be found in the local paper or on the local municipality website.

Bidding on these properties starts at whatever the lienholder is owed so the bidding can be pretty fierce in some instances and still come out to far less than what the property is actually worth. As the information available is going to vary dramatically between auctions, it is important to try and track down as much information about each property as possible as a means of limiting potential risk. Greater rewards come with greater risk, however, and if you are lucky you could easily end up with a property that far exceeds what your budget would otherwise be. It shouldn't be surprising that you need to have cash on hand or a preapproved loan ready to go for these types of auctions as there is no waiting no matter what.

Chapter 4: Negotiating a Deal

The golden rule in real estate is that everything is negotiable, and this is true, up to a point. When you are buying your first real estate investment property you are going to naturally want to get the best deal that you can to maximize your future profits, this doesn't mean you need to haggle over ever last red cent, however, and sometimes knowing when to stop is as important as knowing when to go full bore.

The best way to learn the limits starts with knowing the area surrounding the property as thoroughly as possible, down to the neighborhood and street if possible. First things first, if there are more homes for sale in the area than the local average then this means you are lucky enough to find yourself in a buyer's market. This means you are going to be able to make more demands and even take an extra 10 percent off any offers that you make. If the alternative is true then you are looking at a seller's market which means that you are going to be lucky to pay the asking price and might need to make a few more concessions than you otherwise would.

With so many home listings available online, it can be easy to see the logic in trying to save some extra money by not using a real estate agent during your real estate investment endeavors. It is more difficult than you might expect to get a property successfully from offer to close, however, and there is a lot you can learn from a good real estate agent that makes them worthwhile your first few times out at least. A good agent will also have negotiation experience and insider details about the market that can pull a successful deal together from almost nothing. What's more, as the buyer, you won't be paying for the agent, that will be covered in a commission paid by the seller. When it does come time to try the process yourself, however, consider the following tips to help you start off on the right foot.

Three part process: All successful negotiation can be broken up into three parts, process, behavior, and substance. Process is the way in which you approach a given negotiation, and a confident process can do wonders when it comes to effective negotiations. Substance can be thought of as the details at the heart of the negotiation, and your process should ensure the substance goes in your favor as well. Finally, you can think of the interaction between you and the other party as the behavior of the negotiation.

Do it face to face: When it comes to submitting an offer, you are going to always want to meet with the other party directly if possible. Assuming the market is in your favor, then you are going to have most of the power going into the negotiation and the best way to capitalize on that power is to meet the other person face to face. Alternatively, if the market is currently in the other party's favor you are going to want to negotiate via email instead as this will balance out the power disparity somewhat. When meeting a new seller it is important to listen to the way they say things as well as what is being said. Tonality is actually a combination of two things, volume, and pace. To ensure you get off to a good start with a potential seller you will want to match them on both accounts. This means you are going to want to speak quietly to reserved customers and be brash with those who tend to only use their outdoor voices. A disconnect in either way will make them feel uncomfortable and can potentially cost you the sale as a result.

When you do actually submit your offer, however, you are going to want to do so and then remain completely silent, no matter how long it takes. If the other party also appears to be dead set on not saying anything either, after 90 seconds you can repeat your offer once more. This will limit the other party significantly in terms of how they can proceed, firmly establishing your power in the negotiation even more.

Another reason that you will want to hold the negotiations in person as long as the conditions are favorable is that you can learn a lot about the other person via their body language. If the other submits a counteroffer while using open body language then this means they are more willing to reach a consensus with you. Closed body language, meanwhile indicates that they are not pleased with your original offer and they are less willing to come to an agreement as a result. If they come back with timid body language, however, then this means you likely have them over a barrel and can remain firm.

You are also going to want to make a point of using open body language as well. A defensive, closed body posture automatically tells those around you that you are tense, nervous and unwilling to come to a mutually beneficial agreement. This isn't a secret science either, these are common body language cues that you can bet money on that the seller can read as well, even if this is just subconsciously.

What's worse, once they are aware of them, most sellers will start mimicking them, and their related behaviors as well. Closed body posture gives them the signal that there's something to worry about and they'll fell ill at ease and much more resistant to persuasion. The fix, luckily, is quite simple. If you concerned you may be displaying a defensive body posture, all you need to do is sit up straight so that your spine is aligned, and your shoulders are squared. At the same time, you are going to want to breathe deeply, place your hands on your legs, with your palms up. While this isn't a natural position, it is an important part of the overall whole.

Opening up your posture in this way will also serve to improve your mental state by decreasing the amount of the hormone cortisol that your body produces. Cortisol is responsible for stress levels so in this case acting and outwardly appearing to be calm and collected will make you feel this way as well, relaxing your potential customers in the process.

Consider the market: It is also important to keep the current state of the market in mind as well as this will help set the stage for the entire negotiation. If the market is currently favorable to buyers then you will be able to make additional demands without worrying about the seller backing out. What's even better, you can typically take at least 10 percent off your asking price without losing out. You can even ask the seller to pay the closing costs. On the other hand, if it is currently a seller's market then you will need to be ready to make concessions where appropriate, pay the asking price, and pay the closing costs.

Make the right first impression: Studies show that, statistically speaking, the person who enters the negotiation space with less baggage is going to start off the negation from a greater place of power. Entering the negotiation space should be a streamlined process that makes you look as though you are as ready to get down to business as quickly as possible. Once you start off on the right foot, seize the advantage that it creates with the proper business handshake and a seat that is at a 45-degree angle from the other party to show you are interested in collaborating for everyone's benefit.

Consider your opposition: When it comes to taking stock of the other party in the negotiation, the first thing you are going to want to do is to be aware of the more obvious verbal cues such as erratic gestures, shifty eyes, murmuring, sweating, shaking or excessive blinking are all signs that things are not on the level. While few professional negotiators go about things in such an obvious fashion, you never know what might slip through subconsciously which is why it pays to always keep an eye on the little things.

Other important body language to be on the lookout for includes anything that generates a physical barrier. Common examples of this are crossed arms or holding documents or other props in hand and pressed tightly to the chest. These are all signs that the other person is not receptive to what the other person is saying. In fact, one study looked at more than 2,000 negotiations take place and none of them ended in success if one member never uncrossed their arms.

Regardless of what you find when inspecting the other party, it is important to file it away and use it as a baseline when it comes to determining what affect, if any, your persuasive skills are having. If you instead find the other party to be clearly and obviously ill-prepared this is likely to be a trick. Be on your guard and you are more likely to come out on top regardless of the specifics of the interaction.

Hold eye contact: When it comes to negotiating effectively it is important to maintain eye contact to convey that you trust the other party and are, in turn, trustworthy yourself. You should also make a concentrated effort to increase the amount of eye contact that you are using while you are speaking and use slightly less than normal while the other person is speaking to show that you are in the dominant position and you know it. It is important to break it off before things get too tense, however, as you don't want to take things all the way to aggressive territory.

Pupil constriction and squinting can mean the person is bothered by what they are seeing. A long exhale can mean that the person is under extreme emotional distress. As it is common knowledge that not looking another person in the eyes is a sign of lying, those who lie will often try to overcompensate for this fact which is a great way to determine if they are actually lying after all.

The average amount of eye contact sits at between 7 and 10 seconds in most cultures, during the average conversation, as a sign that both parties are active and committed to the conversation. If the person you are speaking with is holding your gaze in such a way that it makes you want to squirm, resist the urge and instead consider what about the conversation is making them act in such a strange way.

When looking for excessive eye contact, it is also important to pay attention to what the other person's eyebrows are doing as well. Raised eyebrows are typically a sign of discomfort. In fact, raised eyebrows are generally associated with fear, worry or surprise, none of which signal a relaxing conversation with a friend. As such, if you see this automatic response, and it occurs around a topic you wouldn't expect, then you may need to dig a little deeper to determine what exactly is going on.

Play the odds: Statistically speaking, even if it is your first time negotiating a contract, one hundred percent failure is practically impossible to achieve. To that end, if you make a point of running towards instances where you can lowball a seller, you will eventually find one that works out in your favor, guaranteed. While it might take more effort than you would hope for, once you get an extremely good deal once then you will be able to hold onto that memory and it will make it dramatically more likely you will see a second sooner than later. Eventually, you will find that the percentage of times you find it easy to play hard ball during negotiations has swung back around to your favor and from there it will be a simple matter of making it a habit with every property you look at moving forward.

Practice empathy: Empathy needs to become your best friend when you want to negotiate with a seller successfully. Many people think that they have the whole empathy thing down, but any time they are confronted with a situation where they could feel for the other person, they end up failing. People all live different lives, have different troubles, and react differently to the things that go on in their lives. Being able to put yourself in their shoes and understand what is going on can be a big challenge, especially when we are so caught up in our own personal lives. Doing so will ultimately make it easier for you to see the chinks in their armor and find the secret to ensuring the negotiations end up in your favor.

If you are struggling with the whole idea of empathy, it may be time to start working on it a bit more. Start with one person. Make it your goal for the week to think the way that this particular person would in each situation. Instead of acting the way that you would or think that you would react the way that you think they would. This can help you to get a deeper understanding of what is going on with those around you.

Chapter 5: Rental Property Basics

If you are looking for something a little bit more substantial, then you may be interested in a duplex or a small apartment complex with around 6 units or less. Properties with multiple tenants are nice because much more needs to go wrong overall before you suddenly find yourself in a situation where you are not receiving enough to cover the costs of the property in a given month. The biggest concern for these types of properties is the type of tenants who call them home to start as they are going to be one of the most influential factors when it comes to finding future tenants. Depending on the size of the property in question you may even be able to trade property management services in exchange for free board and then you would be able to count on someone being on the premises at all times.

When it comes to renting out a single-family home, you will often find that the easiest way to go about doing so is by using what is known as a turnkey rental property company. So called because the property is completely ready for a renter to move into on purchase, these types of properties require little from you except the initial payment as the company is then in charge of the property management and virtually everything else. As such, it is extremely important that you do your research in this instance otherwise you can easily end up in a bad situation that you are contractually required to follow through on. Additionally, it is extremely important that no matter what you are told you always visit the property in person before committing to everything. Remember, an ounce of prevention is worth a pound of cure.

Rental property considerations: Assuming you plan to do so from the beginning, using a property management company to manage your rental properties creates a passive income opportunity from the moment you close on the property in question. As such, it is important to research property management companies in the area you are planning on purchasing property in to see what their requirements and costs are. Typically, it is difficult to find a property management company for a single, single family home which means a small duplex or fourplex might be the way to go. Alternatively, condominiums are also great for first time investors as they are more likely to attract stable individuals and they come with a built-in property manager as well.

Condominiums are a great choice for a first passive income rental property for several reasons. First, you know there will always be someone on site and you don't even need to worry about paying additional fees for a property manager. Additionally, the types of renters that are looking for condos are typically upwardly mobile professionals which means you will rarely. need to worry about payments being spotty or being made late.

On the other hand, a duplex requires less work than an apartment complex, but more than a condo and it will be important to screen potential renters thoroughly to ensure you don't get stuck paying for the property while dealing with getting someone evicted. Finally, a small apartment complex is nice because you don't need to worry about paying your bills as long as a simple majority of tenants can pay their rent on time. As an added bonus, if you can find a reliable person to be your on premises representation then you might not even need to hire a property management company.

Getting started

Do your homework: Once you have decided on the type of rental property that you are interested in purchasing, the first thing you are going to want to do is to narrow down your search to neighborhoods that are going to attract the interest of the types of tenants you are looking for. If you are planning on purchasing a single-family home, then that means you are going to want to consider areas that have amenities that families are looking for which means things like parks or schools. Meanwhile, if your target renter is instead younger and single then you are going to want to consider local nightlife possibilities.

Regardless of who your target renter might be you are always going to want to consider what the employment options are like in the area, and not just on a superficial level either. Digging deeper to find out if any major companies are planning to move into, or out of, specific areas can often give you a heads up on where the rental market in a specific area is going to be like six months or more down the line.

Do the math: When you come across a property that you are interested in learning more about, the first thing that you will want to do is to run the numbers and ensure that it will work out to be worth your time in the long run. If you aren't sure what you might be able to get for a specific property each month in rent the easiest way to come up with a ballpark number is to simply look at other rental properties in the area and see what the rent is like. With a ballpark number in mind, you can then tweak your personal number based on the property in question and anything that is unique about it.

Rental property tips
Fix it up to a point: After you have found a property in an area that you like for an amount that you can afford to actually pull the trigger on, the next thing you are going to want to do is to get it ready to put on the market. When it comes to getting their first rental property ready for actual renters, it is common for new property owners to go overboard and make the property as impeccable as possible. While going all out is something that your tenants will appreciate, it isn't something that they are willing to pay extra for, however, which is why you are going to want to approach the renovations with a critical eye.

This doesn't mean that you want to leave things in a dank, dangerous or dingy fashion, but it does mean that you don't need to worry about fixing up every nook and cranny. As long as you replace the kitchen cabinets and counters and give the bathroom a bit of a makeover, lots of smaller issues will be accepted by tenants without so much as a peep. Additionally, if your budget is tight, a high likelihood if this is your first rental property, then you can easily hold off on replacing long-term systems until they give out as you are going to be responsible for the repairs or replacements regardless. Finally, when it comes to painting the property you are going to want to stick with something besides white that will work with numerous color palates.

Charge the right amount for rent: Once you find a property that appears as though it meets your needs, the next thing you are going to want to do is to run the potential numbers to ensure it is actually going to be worth it for you to move forward. This means you are going to want to look into the current rental prices for other, similar properties in the area so you can get a basic idea of what's reasonable before factoring in the things that make the property you are looking into unique and adjusting accordingly. Once you have a number in mind, all you need to do is add up the cost that you will pay for insurance, loan payment, property management fees, and taxes and subtract that result from the likely rent amount.

Whatever is leftover is what you as the property owner are going to be entitled to, if it seems like a reasonable number to you then you can go ahead with the property. You will also need to factor in another 10 percent of the total costs to account for any vacancies or missed payments that you can expect to experience now and then. Additionally, you can plan on the property appreciating 3 percent each year, which should be enough to pay for some of the existing fees.

Advertising

Once you have actually finished with a property and it is ready to rent out, the first thing to do is get the word out about it which means taking lots of pictures both inside and out. While you certainly want to show the property in the best light, it is important to not employ any intentionally misleading tactics to make things look better than they are. Doing so will certainly bring in more people but the contrast between the fiction you created and the reality of the property may be enough to turn them off, even if they would have been alright with the flaw in the first place.

When creating online profiles for your rental, it is important to list all the best features of the property in a way that is both clear and succinct. Renters are used to having to wade through piles of useless information to get the details they are looking for so by putting them up front you are sure to grab their attention. When creating your profiles be sure to include things like relation to local schools, public transit options, relation to important local areas, swimming pool, air conditioning, laundry room and anything else that sets the property apart including major renovations you have completed.

Additionally, you will need to clearly present the size of the entire lot as well as the size of the livable space and the policies on things like smoking, deposits, and pets. If time is of the essence and you are looking to get a tenant in the property as quickly as possible without sacrificing long-term profits by simply dropping the rent is to include rent or utilities for a limited time, reduce the amount of deposit that is required or cut the first month's rent by a small portion. While this will certainly cut into your short-term profits, it may be a better solution than letting the property sent empty for a prolonged period of time.

Renting out the property as quickly as possible also means casting as wide of a net as possible which means taking to social media and asking all of your friends to help spread the word as well. Statistically speaking, everyone under the age of 30 is only two degrees of separation removed from someone who is currently looking for or will soon be looking for a new place to live which means a little social media traction is likely all it would take to start seeing real results. Beyond going viral you will not want to underestimate the effectiveness of putting a for rent sign in the front yard which is still how roughly 25 percent of renters found their current residence. You will also want to seek out exclusively regional or local rental services and even the local newspaper can prove a surprisingly effective choice when it comes to attracting new tenants.

A slightly pricier option, though one that is ideal for high quality or niche properties, is to utilize a real estate professional who specializes in the type of property you are looking to rent. If your first rental property is likely to just be the first of many then creating a long-term relationship with someone in this field could lead to years of mutually beneficial business while saving your hundreds of hours in the long-term.

Regardless of your ideal rental plans, it is important to never settle for a subpar tenant (like those discussed in chapter 7) just to prevent the property from sitting empty for a month or two. While it can hurt to have to pay the upkeep on the property while waving goodbye to early profits, the headaches that come along with trying to force out a poor tenant are not something you want to have to deal with if you can possibly avoid it. On the contrary, a good tenant is literally worth their weight in gold and will make it easy for you to ensure your rental property becomes a true passive income stream.

Screening tenants
Once word has gotten out about your new property, it will be time to ensure you find the best possible tenants to keep it looking as nice as is reasonably possible. The screening policy that will be best for you is going to vary from landlord to landlord based on personal preferences, as well as the overall amount of risk you are comfortable dealing with. The most important factor, however, is that you have your specifics in mind and stick to your guns no matter what. As a general rule, however, you should consider the following for your first tenants:

- No previous history of evictions
- Positive references from the previous landlord and current employer
- An acceptable background check which often includes a criminal history clear of misdemeanors and felonies for the previous seven years
- A sum total household income that is three times the total rent when all tenants' income is combined

While you are clearly free to add any additional specifics you might like, you should find that this level of specificity is enough to weed out the types of tenants that are going to cause you problems. When it comes to screening potential renters the process should start with the prescreening which takes place when the potential tenant first sees the property. You should ask them if they meet the requirements that you are going to be looking. This will cut out the honest folks who don't want to waste your time. You should not disqualify them out of hand, however, as an honest tenant is a valuable asset and you should look more closely at the specifics of their situation.

Those who make it through the prescreening phase should then receive an application which will ask for things like relevant personal details, employment information, social security number, and references. If you pull an application from the internet take care to make sure it includes a waiver saying you are allowed to run a background check and a credit check on the applicant for the purpose of determining their eligibility to rent the property.

Background checks can be provided by third-party companies or by the state directly, though specifics will vary by location. You can obtain a credit report on an individual directly from one of the three credit bureaus Equifax, Experian and TransUnion, and this request can be made online. Generally speaking, you should aim for a renter with a credit score of 600 minimum, though something higher might be warranted depending on what you have set the desired rent at.

If you still don't feel quite right about a given applicant after running the checks, this is when you would want to go ahead and call any proffered references, after all, that's what they are there for. When you do make the call you are allowed to ask about anything that is relevant to your decision, as long as it is within reason. If you end up not liking a particular potential tenant then it is legally required that you send them a letter explaining why they were not selected. This is known as a letter of adverse action and it should state what information you gathered and how it affected your decision. You are required to provide this letter within 60 days to anyone whose application you deny.

Chapter 6: Turnkey Rental Properties

A turnkey property is any property that can be purchased with the promise of generating cash flow as quickly as possible, in some cases already with renters attached. There are two primary ways of going about finding a turnkey property to purchase, the first provides greater returns, and the second provides the simplest buying experience possible. First of all, if you are interested in making as much off of a property as possible, your best bet is to find a property that is ready rent out immediately, do the leg work of finding a tenant and then find a property management company who will take you on as a client. Once you have put all of the pieces together yourself, you will find that you manage to retain about 90 percent of the total rental price each month.

Alternatively, you can go through a turnkey property company that specializes in working with investors just like you. In this case, you would only need to choose the company you are interested in working with, pay them for a property and then wait for the profits to roll in. In most instances, you can expect to both pay more for the property up front and also see a smaller return from each month's rent when going this route. On the other hand, in most cases when you purchase a turnkey property from a turnkey company you can expect to start making money back on your investment the very next month.

As you will be planning to hire a professional management company anyway, it is important to understand that the biggest difference between the two is typically going to be how involved you want to be in the process of investment property ownership. While a property management company means you won't have to deal with the property on the regular, issues may arise from time to time that will still require your attention. If you choose to go with a turnkey company the only time you will have to think about your property is when you receive a monthly check in the mail for your part of the profits.

The location that you plan on purchasing a turnkey rental property in will also likely play a part in whether or not you choose to go with a turnkey rental property company over a choose your own property type of approach. Turnkey rental properties are becoming an increasingly popular investment opportunity for those who live in areas where land is scarce, simply because it allows them to easily invest in areas where the property is much more affordable than anything they could ever hope to find locally. Investors looking to set up this type of investment opportunity would naturally gravitate towards a turnkey rental property company simply because it would allow them to know that their property is going to be in good hands even when they are all the way across the country, if not the world.

Choosing a turnkey property company
While the benefit of finding a turnkey property company is that you have to do little more than sit back and wait for the profits to start rolling in, that doesn't mean that is all you ever have to do from day one. Before you reach the point of passive income you are going to want to ensure that you have done plenty of research to ensure that you are going to be ready for everything that the process of finding the right turnkey rental real estate company is going to throw at you.

Separate the wheat from the chaff: When it comes to finding the right turnkey rental real estate company for you, the first thing you are going to want to do is to immediately disqualify any company that doesn't have a physical address and does all of their business through the internet. While the online world has been able to automate many real estate based functions when it comes to a turnkey rental investment you are going to want to know there is some place that you can physically take your complaints to if things do not initially go as planned.

The truth of the matter is that a real, viable turnkey rental property company is going to have a website that is virtually indistinguishable from a fake simply because both are going to show nothing but great looking homes and make promises that you as an investor want to hear. These companies can then easily cash quite a few checks before anyone catches on to the scam and, what's worse, can be in the wind and ready to do it again before anyone even gets close to finding them. Do your rental property investment a favor and treat it with caution, the turnkey rental property company you pick is going to be in charge of your investment completely, treat the choice with the importance it deserves.

Weed out the newer companies: After you have made a point of avoiding any company without a physical location, the next thing that you will need to do is to cross from your list any company that has been in business for less than a decade. The turnkey rental property business is extremely competitive and it takes quite some time to master the intricacies of a particular area; what this means is that if you go with a new turnkey rental property company then you are essentially paying them to learn with your money. Avoid the learning curve entirely, pick a company that is clearly going to know what it is doing because it has been doing it for more than a decade.

The best way to find these types of companies is to look into personal recommendations from someone that you know and trust. Barring a local recommendation, you are going to want to look into the recommendations left by other users online. While a single review, positive or negative, shouldn't sway you one way or another, what you are going to be interested in tracking down are patterns that appear over time concerning the particular turnkey rental property company.

Start with the basics: With the worst of the worst accounted for, the next thing you will need to do is make sure the remaining companies you are looking at have a number of basic things in any reviews you read. For starters, it is important that the company has a long history of success, 10 years minimum. Anything less than this means they might still be working the kinks out of their business or still learning the ropes and you don't want them learning with your money. You will also want to pay special attention to reviews that discuss details that relate to the management or repairs and renovations. Above all, you want to get the feeling that they really are focused on their investors. Verifying this data through a third party is also encouraged.

Reach out to the companies you like the most: Assuming this process has whittled down your list to just a handful of potential candidates, the next thing you are going to want to do is to reach out to each of the companies you are considering in person to see what they are like to deal with. This means you are going to want to track down a phone number, not an email address as you want to know you can call someone directly if an emergency occurs. The more ways a company provides you to get in touch with them, the more likely they are to truly care about receiving customer feedback. Long story short, if any of the companies still on your list only offer email communication then you are going to want to cross them off right away.

When you do reach out to these companies it is important that you wait to see how long it takes them to get back to you and avoid them in the future if it takes them more than 24 hours to return your initial call. After all, if it is clear they don't care about your business right from the start, consider how much worse things are going to be once they already have you under contract. Alternately, they could simply be too busy or too poorly managed to call you back in a timely fashion but these are all signs that you will be better off with another company instead.

Professionalism: Once you have narrowed your list down even more, you will then want to consider how professional the representative you speak with is as this is indicative of the overall level of professionalism of the company as a whole. As someone who is likely not even in the same state as the property you are considering, it is extremely important that you can trust the company you are leaving your investment too and their level of professionalism is a good indication of such.

Likewise, it is important that you can get in touch directly with the person who is managing your property at all times and also that they do more than pay you lip service and go about their day. This means you are going to want to ensure they are never to busy to speak with you or go over some detail of the process, no matter how relatively minor. You should make it a point to come up with excuses to talk to this person multiple times before you sign anything to ensure you have a good measure of what they are really like.

Another important aspect of the company to consider is the level of knowledge the people you speak with have when it comes to their local market as well as the wider market as a whole. By this point in the process, you should already know everything about the area you are considering purchasing property in so it should be relatively straightforward to test their knowledge on the area. Don't be afraid to press them on apparent discrepancies either, they may have more up to date information than you do, after all, and you may end up learning something as well.

Additionally, when you reach out to these companies you should be able to rely on more than their word and your own observations, they should be able to point you towards satisfied customers who can vouch for their level of quality. If you come across a company that is unable to provide you with valid references then you may need to consider why this might be the case. You should also reach out to references with different numbers of rental properties to ensure that no one is getting superior service unduly or based on personal biases.

One area that should be of particular interest is the level of support the company provides after the sale has already been completed. Even if the company has been quite attentive to you so far, having the viewpoint of a person who has already been through the process is vital to ensure that nothing is going to change once the paperwork is signed. Additionally, other investors will be the ones to know if the turnkey company you are dealing with outsources the actual property management duties which means you may need to look into them separately as well.

It is especially important to be aware of this final scenario as this type of setup is not recommended as it often leads to a variety of additional issues before the deal can be closed successfully. If you do decide to go down this route then then it is vital that you do the leg work required to ensure the property management is on the level to avoid needless hassle when you are so close to success.

Consider the pricing: While initially there are any number of reasons why you may be tempted to go after a turnkey property that is priced more competitively than its competition. It is important to avoid this impulse, however, as it will likely end up costing you more in the long-term than you might expect. The research you have done on the area should give you a good idea of what the property in question should go for, and you can bet the company you are looking at knows this as well. As turnkey properties are expected to be at or above market value, the only logical reason this would not be the case then is if something not entirely above board is going on. Whatever it is, the goal of this type of real estate investment is to be as passive as possible and this is a red flag that your experience is going to be anything but straightforward.

Chapter 7: Fulfilling the Role of Landlord

Tenant Types to Avoid

In a perfect world, you, as the landlord, could expect to provide a quality service and, in turn, be treated with respect by a tenant who is eager to make the process as simple for everyone involved as possible. This is rarely the case, however, and if you aren't careful you can find yourself dealing with a tenant that costs you time as well as money. While you will eventually develop a quality screening process that works for you, for now, you will likely find it helpful to keep an eye out for the following types of tenants, so you can avoid them at all costs.

The destructive tenant: There is no type of tenant worse for your newly minted rental property than the destructive tenant. Whether they have a destructive child or pet that they have no control over, remodel a portion of the property to better suit their needs, or are simply not respectful to the property, this type of tenant is likely to cause extreme damage to your property and then try and do their best to get you to pay for it.

Luckily, it is often possible to pick out a destructive tenant when they come to look at the property, as long as you think to look for the signs. First, you are going to want to be sure to meet them by their vehicle as its condition will often give you a good idea of what you can expect when your property is under their care. If they have children, then you will want to pay attention to how well-behaved they are. The children don't need to be perfect, they are children after all, but there is a big difference between a normal child and one that is willfully destructive. Regardless of how they present themselves during the walkthrough, you will always want to call the previous landlord and ask about the state of the property when the tenant moved out.

The tenant who is loud: Tenants who are excessively noisy can be some of the most frustrating for a landlord to deal. While they are unlikely to cause much damage by themselves, this type of tenant practically ensures that you or your property manager are going to get calls from the neighbors on the regular requesting that you do something about your unruly tenant. If the neighbors skip this step and go right to the police then you may have the authorities requesting that you reign in your tenant as well. This issue is often made all the worse by the fact that when you and the tenant interact they are extremely friendly and always pay the rent on time. Regardless, once the calls start rolling in on the regular you are sure to regret this decision immensely.

What's more, disqualifying a loud tenant can be difficult, regardless of how easy it can be to spot them up front. Signs of a loud tenant include things like stories about rowdy friends, questions about extra outlets for surround sound, questions about the neighbors' attitudes towards parties and similar things are all strong signs that a tenant might make life uncomfortable for you and the neighbors both. Instead, the best way to deal with this potential problem is to point out what the rest of the neighborhood is like and point out that they have your phone number as well. If this doesn't work then you will need to find another reason to legally disqualify them from the property.

The tenant that doesn't pay rent: While dealing with a destructive tenant is never fun, as long as you received their deposit and they pay their rent on time there is little they can do that cannot be undone. That is why the absolute worst type of tenant is the one that uses every excuse under the sun to justify why they are going to be late on the rent and then stretch that timeframe out as long as possible. This is rarely the first time this type of tenant has found themselves "a little short" this month and they have likely learned over time what they can get away with under the law which means they will almost always owe you something.

Luckily, this type of tenant leaves a trail that is typically quite easy to follow as long as you do your homework. This is why it is so important to always run a credit check on every applicant and also get, and verify, their residency history. This is also why you want to have a firm policy in place when it comes to previous evictions as if it has happened before then there is a good chance it could happen again which is more than enough reason to steer clear all on its own.

Sure, sometimes an otherwise good tenant may end up in an untenable situation and have no choice but to go through the eviction process, but when it comes to your first few rental properties you likely won't be able to take that chance which is why sticking to this rule is so important. Always do your due diligence before letting anyone put any money down, you only have yourself to blame by the results if you don't.

The tenant that will have too many animals: While deciding to allow pets in a property is something you will need to consider for yourself, there is a difference between a tenant with one small dog and half a dozen dogs plus as many cats. This is why it is important to have a pet policy in place and do what you can to ensure it is strictly enforced. Unfortunately, this is easier said than done which is why it is important to always check with the previous landlord to see what type of shape the previous property was left in when they vacated. If a previous landlord complains about pets then there is no reason to assume this will not be an issue again in the future. While this may not be enough to disqualify the tenant on its own, it should be enough that you are looking for other reasons to disqualify them.

The lying tenant: The difficulty that a lying tenant will cause is directly proportional to the type of lies they are telling. A tenant that lies about having steady employment but who regularly freelances and can thus pay the rent is one thing, a tenant that lies about being an intravenous drug user is quite another. Unfortunately, even with a tenant who starts off with mild lies, you can often anticipate that they will lie about other things like the state of the property when they moved in or when they move out if it suits them.

Sorting out the liars is one of the more difficult things to do as a landlord as you will have very little information to go off of. This means it is important to pay as close of attention to all the details you do have as possible in order to keep an eye out for anything that might be a bald-faced lie. A lie at this stage should thus be unforgivable as it is the only indication you will get that this type of behavior is something you may have to deal with again in the future.

The party tenant: This is another type of tenant whose tendencies are fine in moderation but intolerable after a certain point. The definition of a tenant that throws a party now and then and one that parties too much is going to vary based on the type of property and where it is located. Too much partying can disrupt the flow of a neighborhood and can lead to drunk and disorderly conduct, fighting, vandalism and more, not to mention illegal behavior of one type or another is virtually guaranteed after a certain point.

Luckily, as long as you don't plan on being too strict, it should be relatively easy to determine right from the start if a tenant is going to fit in with the neighborhood your property is a part of. Checking with their landlord and personal references is a great place to start and this, plus a background check should give you the details you need to determine if they like to take things a bit too much to the extreme for your liking.

The tenant who enjoys too much drama: While most renters want nothing more than to fly under the radar of their landlord until their lease is up, others will only be happy if they are always dealing with some type of issue that needs to be resolved ASAP. These issues usually manifest themselves as a constant barrage of phone calls either following up on a previous issue or informing you about some new emergency. Whatever their favorite reason for calling, you can bet you will be tempted to block their number before everything is said and done.

Weeding out this type of applicant can be difficult at first but is sure to grow easier with a little practice. An easy way to spot this type of tenant is that they are often extremely eager during the walkthrough, taking note of every nook and cranny, especially anything that they feel will have to be fixed before they can move in. They could also be extremely curious about the neighbors and the level of crime in the area. If you feel as though you may be dealing with a dramatic tenant then making it clear that you will not play into their game should be enough to get them to move on.

The tenant that is extremely entitled: A majority of the tenants you deal with over the years will inevitably understand that a tenant/landlord relationship is one of give and take. Now and then, however, you will come across the type of tenants that believe just because they are paying you rent means you are entitled to give them the world in order to make them happy. This is not the tenant that nicely asks that you come out and fix their broken water heater, it is the type of tenant that will insist you come out in the middle of the night because their faucet has sprung a leak. These sorts of tenants will not only make it their mission to make your life miserable from the moment they move in until the day they move out, they will feel it is their right to do so.

Luckily, as long as you are paying attention, this type of tenant is one of the easiest to pick out from the start. Throughout the walkthrough, they are going to be the ones not just pointing out existing issues but demanding that you fix them before they could even begin to move in. They won't have valid things to say about the property either, they will find issue in things that 90 percent of renters would overlook without thinking twice.

The tenant that knows too much: While it may be difficult to disqualify them, you are also going to want to keep an eye out for the type of renter that is overly familiar with the renter laws in your state. Paralegals, lawyers and the like often know just how far they can push things and still stay within in the law. While this will inherently mean that things will never get too out of hand, it will certainly be annoying for the entire length of the lease as they exploit loopholes for personal gain. While this is far from a guarantee, when it comes to your early rentals you want the process to go as smoothly as possible from start to finish.

Writing a lease
Once you have found a tenant that you can deal with, the final thing you will need to consider is the lease that you will write to ensure that your new tenant knows exactly what your expectations are when it comes to the property. It doesn't matter how obvious or outrageous you think specific actions might be, if you don't outline it clearly in your lease then you can expect at least one tenant to eventually try and do it. What's more, as a general rule you can expect tenants to follow rules that are clearly explained upfront and in writing, than they are

those that are discussed in person or after they have already moved in. In writing also ensure that they understand exactly what the consequences for breaking the agreed upon rules will be.

Again, it is of the upmost importance that you have a clear list of consequences when it comes to what will happen if the tenant goes outside your wishes and breaks the rules. More importantly, having everything written down and signed up front will make it easier for you to take appropriate legal action against tenants that do not follow the rules. What follows is a list of recommendations that make for a good starter lease for those who don't have anything specific in mind.

When rent should be paid: It is important to make it clear both what day the rent is due on as well as what the tenant can expect to happen if they are late. Giving the tenant an extra day or so is nice but certainly not required. Likewise, it is important to clearly state what the late fees will be like if the rent is not paid on time. Common options are either a percentage of the rent or a fixed amount for each day the rent is late.

When you are allowed on the property: It is equally important that you make it clear the various reasons and times you may enter the property. Generally speaking, this will be either with justifiable cause or if you give 24-hour warning first.

Disposal of waste: While this shouldn't be necessary, the sad truth is that it is important to make it clear to the tenant that they have to regularly take out their trash and how frequently they must do so. Not only is this a hygiene issue, if your property has too much trash on it then you can be fined be the city which is why it is important to make it clear what you expect in regard to this issue.

The overall state of the property: In order to protect yourself and your property it is important to make it clear that the renter needs to do what they can be reasonably expected to do in order to ensure the property stays in close to the same condition that you found it in. If they fail to do so then you also need to make it clear that you will be keeping their deposit if they don't hold up their end of the bargain. This clause should apply both in the home and on the property in general. You also need to make it clear what will account for natural wear in your opinion to ensure things are as crystal clear as possible.

Pets: Do you allow pets or not? Many of the large apartment complexes owned by real estate investment groups and REITs do not allow pets. They are unwilling to lose the profit it takes to clean an apartment after a pet has been inside. There is also a higher chance for multiple units to be empty at the same time.
If apartment complexes allow pets, the fees are astronomical. A renter may pay as much as $400 for a pet deposit, per pet. They may also be charged with pet rent per month, which can be anywhere from $10 to $100 a month, per pet. A person really has to love their pets to want to pay a high price. There is also an issue of how many pets one can have. Typically, the maximum is two. There are also breed and size restrictions in many apartment complexes. When a person moves out, if the unit needs a deeper cleaning because their pet left an odor or there was damage to doors/walls, then they lose their entire deposit. This is why some apartment complexes have weighed the risk of having pets against the costs they incur and decline to allow pets.

For a person with a single property, trying to rent it, there are other considerations to be made.

1. If a pet damages the carpet, you either need to have it cleaned or rip it out and replace it.
2. If damage occurs to the door trim, doors, window trim, tile, or other flooring due to the pet, you have to fix it.
3. You are usually renting a property in a neighborhood, which may not be happy if a loud animal continually makes noise throughout the day and night.
4. You may lose more than 50% of the possible renters who are looking for a property.

If you decide to allow pets, you should have a strict pet policy that is maintained. For example, if you allow cats and dogs, you should outline how many pets total can be in the property, if there are any breeds you will not allow, and if there are any weight restrictions. The more detailed your pet policy, the easier it will be to bring a renters attention to it when or if it is broken.

You can also ask for a deposit that includes enough to cover cleaning up after pets.

The deposit
Always get a deposit. You can legally request first and last month's rent, as well as a deposit. It will depend on how much the rent is and the area you are trying to rent in. The "last" month's rent can be seen as a deposit too but be clear what can and cannot happen when someone moves out, with regards to the deposit.

Chapter 8: Property Flipping Basics

Fix and flip is the colloquial term for purchasing a less than desirable property, fixing it up, and selling it for a profit. While this can be an extremely time-intensive undertaking if you go it alone, the next few chapters will also discuss putting together a team to ensure the process is as streamlined as possible. While it can be difficult to get started with, if you stick with it in the long-term then you will find that you can make a tidy sum when everything is said and done.

Basics

ARV: When looking for properties that the meet the fix and flip criteria the number one thing you will need to consider for every property is what its After Repair Value (ARV) is. The ARV is the amount that you can expect to sell the property for when everything is said and done and it has been renovated successfully. It is very important to work out the ARV on a property as soon as you find out about it as overestimating this number at the moment could lead to a loss in the long run.

To divine the ARV for a specific property you will need to start with an estimate relating to what you feel you can get the property for out the door. From there, you will want to add in the cost of the renovations, as well as any other costs that will need to be considered while the property is in your hands. An acceptable ARV is no more than 70 of what you believe you can realistically sell the property for in a reasonable period of time. If the property you are considering doesn't meet these standards then you will have no choice but to move on as it is not really worth the effort.

Having a firm ARV in mind needs to be something that you do before you go for the initial property visit as it will ensure you don't get unduly invested in a property that will ultimately go nowhere. While this rule might seem needlessly strict at first, you will find that if you shift it by as much as five percent you start to see serious losses, especially if you end up underestimating the true cost of the renovations.

Think about who will buy the property: When looking at any property and determining the ARV it is also important to take into account the type of person that you expect to purchase it once it is fixed up and on the market. Doing so will make it far easier to decide how much work actually needs to be done as well as what you will likely be able to sell the property for. For example, if you are looking for properties in rural areas then things like extra rooms are important in the outbuildings because the new owners are likely going to want extra space for toys as well as animals. It is also important to know what types of animals the property is zoned for as you can bet someone is bound to ask. Alternately, if you are looking in the suburbs then things like good schools and other family focused amenities bring in premium prices which is why you will want to look at homes with lots of bedrooms and bathrooms.

Regardless of the type of property you are considering, there is money to be made, no matter what the layout may be, as long as you have a clear idea who you are going to try and sell the property to from the start. Focusing on the strengths of the property will not only reduce the need for excessive remodeling, but it will also help you sell the property quickly as well.

Look for added value: When making improvements to a property it is important to keep a very close tally on the value you bring in along the way. It is also a good idea to take pictures with each step as this will but into sharp focus how much work you actually put in as a means of successfully justifying your asking price. This does not mean that you will need to completely renovate the properties that you purchase as you are only going to want to touch the things that are going to directly improve the price of the property as a whole. More specifically, this means you are rarely ever going to want to undertake projects such as enlarging a living room or putting in a completely new kitchen unless the existing rooms are in such poor shape that the property will not sell otherwise. If you want to turn a profit when everything is said and done then keeping the bottom line in the front of your mind should always be your top priority.

When it comes to decorating and design decisions you are going to always want to stick with neutral colors with the exception of pure white. With every choice you make you should be striving to be as inclusive as possible in terms of potential accent styles as you will want as many different people to be able to picture their own possessions in the space as possible. Everyone who walks in should be able to feel at home in the space and aggressive colors and styles will only limit these possibilities.

Get educated: You cannot locate a cheap house online, purchase the house, and then sell for profit. If it was that easy to flip, everyone in the world would be billionaires. You must be educated before you begin to look at houses. What is it you need to know?

- Understand the ins and outs of your local market. What areas are people buying in right now? What type of house are they buying? Do not look at the new neighborhoods. You want to get the house sold fast.
- Make sure you understand all of your financing options. Are you going to purchase with cash? Are you going to have to get a mortgage loan, or get a home equity line of credit? Make sure that you understand how financing works before you apply for it.
- Have skills when comes to finding good deals. Do research on plumbing, electrician, and landscaping rates. Know the amount it will cost to re-carpet a house. You should know all of this to make sure you find all of the best deals.
- Talk to buyers and do extensive networking before you even start thinking about house flipping. Make sure you do the best you can to build a good relationship with potential buyers. Try having a buyer read when you buy a house; the house will sell when the updates get completed.
- Find a mentor. If you know someone who has successfully flipped houses, ask them to be a mentor. You could also offer then an incentive for their help. You could give them a percentage of your first profit for their advice and knowledge. They will be more motivated to tutor you and make sure you get a quality education. Offering an incentive will enable you to approach others that you do not know since you are going to be compensating them for their efforts.

Overall renovation tips
Start by breaking every required task down as much as possible: While it can be stressful to think of everything that needs to be done to get a property show ready, especially if you picked it up cheap because it needed a lot of work, you will find that it is helpful to break every task down into its primary components. Not only will this make it easier for you to determine what projects you or your friends and family can take care of without professional help, but it will help make all of those tasks seem more manageable as well.

If you are planning on doing as much of the project yourself as possible, and it is your first time tackling this sort of thing then your best bet is to typically start in the laundry room, where available. The reasons for this are two fold, first, the room is typically on the small side and there likely won't be all that much that needs to be done with the space outside of cleaning and maybe a new coat of paint which means you can use a small success to bolster your confidence moving forward. Even better, if things don't exactly break your way, then you have only botched one of the least important rooms in the house instead of something high value like the bathroom or the kitchen.

Don't overestimate the little things: While they can easily add significant value to a property, many new real estate investors get so focused on the bigger issues that need to be taken care of that they often let the little things go repair. Little things like old outlet covers, dirty fans, old fixtures, chipped doorframes all add up to your detriment, however, which means you are going to want to ensure these things are gone over specifically before you start showing the property.

Chapter 9: Building the Right Team

When you're doing your primary research about how much money you need in order to purchase a property, it's not enough to simply think about the down payment. You're going to want to also consider other factors including taxes, inspection fees, and most importantly the cost of repair. If you're more of the business type and not really the hands-on repairman or repairwoman type, you are more than likely going to have to contract the repairs that you need to get done to other people.

If you have to contract all of the work that needs to be done on the house, you're going to be spending a small fortune on fixing it up and this does not bode well for your profit margin. This is often the reason why handymen will invest their time and energy into flipping property, and this is known in the business as "sweat equity".

If you're someone who is naturally good at putting up drywall, laying tile, and installing products that need to be done by a plumber, then you are going to be saving money on the cost that it would otherwise take to have a professional come in and do this for you. If you don't have the skillset to take on these types of tasks, the next best thing is to develop an arsenal of people who will accomplish these tasks for you on the cheap. Often, if you can guarantee these types of people that you will have consistent work for them to do over a long period of time, they will be more likely to offer you some sort of deal in exchange for their services.

Unfortunately, building the right sort of team can be more difficult than you might hope while also costing more than you likely think you can afford. Luckily, having them in place means that once the property sells successfully you can then pay everyone out while still keeping a decent amount of the profits for yourself. While doing everything yourself will always result in a larger profit, it will also take much longer so that by the time you finish one property by yourself, you and your team could have done three whole projects. This is, of course, assuming you can find team members who are willing to do the work up front, with an understanding of what the payment arrangement is going to be.

Assuming you don't have the funds to front the renovation costs up front, this is going to be the first thing you are going to want to consider. Once more, a local real estate investment club in an invaluable resource in this scenario as members can often point you in the right direction. A personal referral also means you know that you can count on work being done on time and to the standard of quality you would hope for, especially when compared to the hit or miss nature of online referrals.

Support staff: While a traditional real estate agent will likely be willing to work with you when it comes to finding the types of properties that you are looking for; for a small cut of course, for the best results, you are going to want to seek out an independent REO real estate agent. An REO agent is different from a more traditional real estate agent in that they specialize in homes that are in bank foreclosure. While finding an REO agent will likely take a bit longer, the end result will be more than worth the extra effort as you will have access to a far superior range of properties as a whole. Real estate agents who are known to specialize in short sales are also worth keeping an eye out for. These individuals are much rarer than traditional real estate agents but all the work you will likely do tracking them down and building a positive relationship will be returned 10 fold in the quality types of properties they will provide you access to.

The next two people you will need to find for your team are going to be a certified public account who specializes in real estate and an attorney who does the same. While these folks are sure to charge a fair amount for their services, in this instance you will very much get what you pay for. If the time comes and you ever need their services in more than a superficial way you will be extremely happy to have them in your corner. Looking for a local recommendation from a real estate club or a trusted mentor is recommended but keep in mind their fees are likely not as fixed as they may like you to think so there is often a little wiggle room if you ask nicely.

While a real estate lawyer shouldn't be hard to find, locating a CPA with real estate experience might be trickier, especially in smaller towns. Perseverance is important in this instance, however, as the tax code can easily be interpreted in a wide variety of different ways which means that there is often an interpretation that works out in your favor, if only you know the person to find it for you. it is also important to ensure your lawyer and your CPA work well together as they will hopefully be seeing each other regularly. You will want them both to make sure your business plan for each new property is up to snuff as well.

Contractor: Once you have a quality support team in place, you can move on to the person you will be working most closely with on your flipping venture, your contractor. While you may be able to handle smaller projects on your own, assuming you are relatively handy that is, on anything larger you will be far better served by letting the professionals handle it as what you pay in additional expenses you will be able to more than make up for with the increased rate you will be able to get your properties to market. This is why it is important to choose not just one contractor, but two in case the first does not work out.

The reason the general contractor is so important is that they are the one who essentially runs the project. They will often come with their own team of subcontractors as well who you will be free to use or dismiss as you see fit. Finding a good contractor does require some legwork, however, which is why it is recommended that you follow the steps outlined below for the best results.

1. The first step to successfully finding a subcontractor involves finding recommendations. If you don't have a local real estate club to ask about such things then you will want to check with local real estate agents to see who they use. Along similar lines, building inspectors are another good source of information as they are sure to remember the names of the people who have worked on the best projects they've seen. What's more, building relationships with both of these types of folks is almost sure to pay off somewhere down the line. Finally, stopping at local lumber mills and asking after contractors that always buy the highest-quality products will often generate some leads as well.

2. After you have your starter list of names, the next thing you are going to want to do is to conduct a round of phone interviews in order to save yourself from having to meet face to face with those contractors who obviously aren't going to work out. Important questions to ask during the interview include things such as:
   - What type of projects are they comfortable with?
   - How many projects do they work on at once?

- Would they be able to wait for payment until the property sells?
- Are they able to provide references?

3. With that out of the way, you will then want to meet with the best candidates and get to know then a little better as you will be spending a fair amount of time with them moving forward. You will also want to discuss your future plans in detail, as well as get a general estimate for the job on any properties you currently have your eye on, just for reference.

4. Finally, you will want to follow up on the references for any of the candidates that managed to make it this far. This is one of the most important steps in the process as you are putting a lot of trust in this person and need to know that they are going to follow through with their side of the bargain.

Subcontractors: Even though your general contractor trusts the chosen subcontractors, that does not mean that you have to trust them, too. It is a good idea to get to know your subcontractors before they begin working on your home. Ask for samples of their work and find out from your contractor why he or she likes them so much. If there is something that you do not like, consider trying to find other ones. Your general contractor will likely have contacts with other people who will be able to help you find subcontractors who are just perfect for your investment property.

All subcontractors should have samples of the work that they have done. They should be willing to show them to you. It is a good idea to do a quick check of their credentials before you make the decision to allow your general contractor to hire them to work on your project. You never know what may be lurking under the surface of what seems like a great business. Make sure that they are efficient at what they do, too. You don't want your entire project to be held up because your plumber doesn't even know how to install a new commode.

Something that you may not know is that you can hire your general contractor without accepting the work of his or her chosen subcontractors. You need to be happy with all of the work that is being done on your home and if the subcontractors are not providing that to you, feel free to fire them and replace them with a company that you like better. Just because the general contractor that you have hired likes a certain company does not mean that you will need to use that company for your project. Your general contractor should understand that you would prefer to use someone that you like better.

Chapter 10: Selling the Property

Marketing: Marketing has changed in recent years. In fact, ever since the internet became a public entity, the real estate world changed. Real estate gurus had the idea of starting various sites that post available listings, which makes your work slightly easier. Clients can look online at listings and then contact the listing agent to inquire about the property. It can also make things a little harder because the listing agent is the name that appears on the MLS details.

The listing agent can be contacted directly, so that cuts out the need for two agents to be part of the deal. Although certain things have become a little difficult, other aspects of marketing have become somewhat easier.

Here are avenues you should explore for marketing:
- Social media, including LinkedIn, Facebook, Twitter
- Real Estate Websites: Realtor.com, Zillow.com, etc.
- Creating your own website
- Putting a page on the business website (if you house your office in another real estate office)
- Business cards
- Joining real estate investment groups/clubs
- Real Estate seminars
- Renovation (fix and flip) seminars
- Blogging on WordPress.com
- Writing or having a real estate book written for Kindle

These suggestions are going to help you get your name out there. You still market in old fashioned means, such as phone books, newspapers, and other similar media. However, you want to make sure the bulk of your marketing is through networking resources and online resources. Utilizing these avenues will give you a chance to access more people, gain referrals, and make your business more successful.

It will still take time for the first sale to happen, but at least you are doing all that you can with networking and marketing for real estate sales. Your reputation in the business is going to matter. Make sure you keep your integrity, not only among clients, but among others in the same business as well.

Ensure the house is in the best shape possible
First and foremost, it is going to be likely that the sellers of the property are going to look to you to tell them what they need to do in order to get their property into the best shape possible. Consider making them a checklist with the following listed on it.

Timing your Open House: Open houses are best on Friday, Saturday, and Sunday. This gives one weekday for a person to see the house if they work weekends. Weekends are when most people are free, but not all. Another option if you work in a neighborhood that has many people working weekends, is to stage an evening open house. You can catch them after work any day of the week.

Make sure you are not hosting an open house when there is a festival, sports game, big concert, or other big events that would draw your potential buyers away. Most people need a house, but they are more apt to choose an event that is not recurring versus an open house that could be scheduled on a different day.

Start with a good first impression: The first impression that a property offers can literally make or break a sale in the first 30 seconds. It is important to stress this to sellers as a way to get them to freshen up things like the exterior paint or landscaping. Ensure they include an easy to see address, remove vehicles from the driveway and clean and remove all clutter as well.

Hire professional cleaners: No matter how motivated a seller is, odds are a professional is going to get things cleaner than they ever could. While some sellers will balk at the cost, it is important to stress how important a spic and span property is its overall appeal during the showing.

Less is more: If the property that you have been enlisted to help sell is absolutely full of things like furniture or knickknacks, then it will be in your best interest to convince the seller to move some of the clutter to another location to give the property a chance to breath. The goal should be for the property to not look barren, but to be on the minimalist side of the spectrum without a doubt. The same goes for wall or floor coverings, potential buyers like to see what they are getting. Keep accent pieces, and mirrors on the walls to open up closed spaces but keep it simple.

Making a good impression: before anyone enters your home, they are going to see the front door, any front yard, and the exterior of the home. The exterior door should be painted, if there are any chips, scratches, or peeling paint issues. Your client will need to freshen up the landscaping, and cover over the main bruises on the exterior paint. The garage door, if there is one, needs to be cleaned if not repainted. A new mailbox or a painted one needs to welcome potential buyers.

Remove personal items: personal items will take away from the potential buyer's sight. They will see family photos and other personal items that detract from the potential of the house. What they want to see is a mantle over the fireplace that is empty, where they can envision their own pictures. They also want to see a clean fridge, where they know there is no dirt, dent, or personal images.

Lock pets in a specific area: if your client has pets make certain the pets are out of the way. It is best to have the animals out of the house, but if there is no option, then they should be in an unimportant room. If at all possible, the pets should be outside or taken with the client for the time the open house will be ongoing. This way potential buyers can open doors, without worry that a pet will escape or be locked in a closet.

Set up signs: You will want to have signs up on the main street, at any turn the potential buyer needs to make, and at the house. The more signs that are visible the easier it will be to get people into the house.

Advertising: How do you advertise real estate? You cannot rely on a sign in the front yard of a property. There must be other ways that you can generate sales and gain potential clients.

- Social Media: Social media is not only a way to get your listings out there and network, but it is also a way for you to advertise. Create ads that provide an advertisement of your skills, as well as profile pages that tell people about yourself.

- YouTube Videos: Videos work in targeting select clientele. Investors are often looking for video tutorials and potential property to purchase. Sellers need tips on how to stage their home. Buyers want a virtual walk through of a home. Videos are a perfect way to give everyone what they want. Make the video funny, insightful, and educational. It should be no more than a minute, whether it advertises a listing, who you are, or your business.

- Write Effective Ad Copy: If you are not a writer, hire one. You need a writer who can create listings that sell properties. You also need a writer who can create ad copy. It is important to tell a story about a property to appeal to the buyer's emotions, as well as providing the reader with the facts.

Chapter 11: Property Wholesaling

If you are interested in the active investment nature of property flipping but don't want to have to worry about the part in the middle when renovations are actually done before making a profit, then property wholesaling may be the real estate investment strategy for you. The basic property wholesale transaction proceeds thusly, first, you find a property that you know could be flipped for a profit, next you negotiate the price of the property to a point that you and another investor can both make money on it and then you sell the property for a profit.

Before you go out trawling for properties to wholesale, you will need to keep in mind what your particular state has to say about wholesaling as different states see it differently and have different laws in place to regulate the practice. The laws you are going to want to definitely check into relate to how your state feels about brokering. Generally speaking, as the person who found the buyer and the seller of a given property transaction that would make you the broker in this situation. If your state considers you a broker for wholesaling, then you are going to need to find out if brokers in your state are required to have real estate licenses, as many do. If your state considers wholesaling a form of assigning a contract, then it is unlikely that you will be required to have a real estate license to do so. Regardless, the best course of action is to simply schedule some time with a real estate lawyer who can set you straight.

If you live in a state that does require you to get your real estate license in order to officially wholesale properties, you can either proceed down that route which will have multiple ancillary benefits for your real estate investment career, or if you are anxious to get started, you can instead perform essentially the same process via what is known as a double close. To perform a double close, you are going to need two willing individuals, the original seller and the ultimate buyer, to work with you in tandem to ensure things are done in a legal fashion. To start, you and the primary seller agree to a contract and wait for the deal to close, meanwhile, you then stagger a second deal with the ultimate buyer, agree to a contract, and wait for that deal to close a few days after the first. You then use the funds from the second transaction to pay for the first.

Ensuring that this type of double deal is possible often comes down to the type of contract that the primary seller is willing to enter into with you and any issues they are currently abiding by relating to encumbrance. Encumbrance is any one of several types of claims that limits how the property can be transferred while also limiting its free use until the encumbrance related issue has been dealt with. The various types of easements that you may have to deal with when wholesaling properties are outlined below.

Easement: An easement can either be used to allow another person to improve a property that they do not own, or it can be used to prevent the owner of a property from improving it in specific ways. If you come across this type of encumbrance you are going to need to see it resolved before most flippers will even touch it in case the easement prevents them from making the changes they need to if they want to make a profit on the property. Additionally, depending on the type of property that you are dealing with, you may need to negotiate easement rights that do not come along with the original contract. If, for example, you purchase a property which draws its water from a well located on another person's property based on an easement that is already in place then the water rights would not, necessarily, transfer along with the property itself.

Encroachment: An encroachment easement relates to instances such as property lines disputes which can lead to secondary issues like issues with trespassing or nuisance in regard to what were assumed to be pre-existing usage rights. If left unresolved this can lead to encumbrance being placed on the property until the issue is resolved.

Lease: If you are planning to purchase a property that currently has some type of lease on it then you will be encumbered until that lease is up unless you are able to work out some agreement with the tenant or transfer the agreement to the lease along with the title of the property.

Lien: If you are looking at property that has a lien associated with the title then this means the previous owner either defaulted on a loan or used the land as collateral in another loan that was then defaulted on. This means the creditor is allowed to sell their land as a way of recouping their losses. A lien can also be placed on a piece of property by the government if the previous own owed unpaid taxes. Finally, a lien can be placed on a property if serious work was done to the property that was not paid for and the judge rules in favor of the person who did the work.

Making an offer

Once you have a property in your sites, the next step will be to determine what is known as the maximum allowable offer which is the most you can pay for the property while still turning a profit. This amount can be found by taking the ARV and subtracting out what the person buying the property from you is going to expect to make on it. From there you will also want to subtract out the renovations costs, as well as any other costs. Finally, you will need to decide what you need to make the transaction and from there you will end up with your maximum allowable offer.

While the easiest way to come up with accurate estimate for each of these numbers is going to be experience, plain and simple, finding a general contractor who is willing to visit properties and help you estimate the potential cost of repairs is a good place to start as if you pay attention you should be able to get the basics down relatively easily. As always, a local real estate club is a good place to start looking for this type of person.

If this does not appear to be an option, you can also research the potential ARV of given properties in an area based on the list of criteria that you devise, though it often takes more time to get up and running using this method. You could also start by befriending a real estate agent and shadowing them to determine the ARV of the properties they work with. Finding an agreeable real estate agent should be easy with a few tries, you will also find another outlet to search for new and potentially profitable properties. Don't forget, the importance of a good team cannot be overstated.

Maximizing the contract's potential: Once you have a signed contract ready to go, one of the last things you need to do is to find a seller that you know will purchase the property for a price that you will be able to turn a profit on. There are a variety of buyer types you can choose from, though ideally, you will want to locate a cash buyer. A cash buyer is a real estate investor who has collected enough funds to ensure they have cash on hand for any properties they want to purchase. In fact, a majority of the more successful property flippers you meet are likely to fall into this category. Cash buyers are ideal because they will allow you to transfer the contract and walk away with your earnings on the same day.

While you might not think that there are lots of folks out there with $100,000 or more burning a whole in their pockets, the fact of the matter is that if you have done your job up to this point and managed to get the property for a price you can profit from then you should be able to find someone who will take it off your hands. As you might expect, the best place to find these types of individuals will be at a local real estate investment club and if no one in the club fits the bill then they can likely point you in the right direction.

Once you have a small stable of cash buyers on hand you very likely won't need to find any more as three or four could very well be enough to set you up for life. You can develop a mutually beneficial relationship with these individuals if you play your cards right and establish working relationships that last decades. With this out of the way, all you need to do is take your share of the profits and be on your way. Many property wholesalers falter at this point, however, because they get greedy and try and upsell their properties an excessive amount. This is shortsighted, however, as the benefits of being reasonable far outweigh the extra profit you will make in the short-term.

Chapter 12: REITs

If you are interested in the idea of investing in real estate but don't like the idea of dealing with the trouble of finding a rental property to purchase, then investing in Real Estate Investment Trusts (REITs) might be more your speed. With this passive income stream, you don't need to worry about having lots of cash already on hand for a large down payment and can get started with virtually any amount. This is because when you invest in REITs you are investing in individual shares the same way you would as if you were investing in a company via buying into their stock. This means, instead of worrying if a given property is ultimately going to turn a profit, all you need to do is choose a REIT that has a proven track record and let their team of analysts make profitable decisions for you. In return for your investment, you will receive dividends just as you would if you invested in dividend producing stocks.

Investing in REITs does have its own drawbacks, however, as it typically requires you to pay taxes on the dividends you receive in addition to paying taxes on the income used to purchase your shares in the first place. If you are hoping to generate passive income as a retirement strategy, however, then you can negate this double taxation by putting the money into an IRA account and agreeing not to touch the funds until you are ready to retire.

REITs were created in the 1960s as a way for the average working individual to partake in the profits generated by larger real estate investments such as hotels and major office complexes, to that end they are required to ensure that 90 percent of their profits return to the shareholders and that more than five individuals control 50 percent of the available shares. Additionally, if you don't approve of the current direction of the REIT then you are free to get rid of your shares freely on the open market at any time without taking any type of penalty. Share prices fluctuate just like stock prices do so you can make the right choice for you at any time.

Choosing a REIT: When it comes time to choose the REIT that is right for you, the first thing you are going to want to do is plenty of research. Luckily, as you will soon see most REITs are pretty self-explanatory when it comes to their holdings which means you can often go and visit them yourself in order to see if everything appears to be on the up and up. Additionally, you will be able to look up their historical dividend yields, with 7 percent being the goal to shoot for. You will also want to consider the amount of growth it has seen for the past few years which can be determined by looking into their net income and operation funds from which you can determine their year over year cash flow. You are going to want to choose a REIT that has at least a 5 percent average growth range per year.

Another useful statistic to track is the number of the REIT's shareholders are institutional investors. Institutional investors include things like investment firms and other professional investment organizations which means that the more institutional investors a REIT has, the greater the odds that it is going to perform as anticipated. Last but not least, when it comes time to price out individual shares, you are going to want to focus on REITs that are in your budget, but at the same time are not budget priced. Shares that are priced to move are a sure indication that the REIT that is offering them has either just been through some rough times or that it expects rough times ahead, and either way it is a proposition that you should want no part of.

Equity REITs

Equity REITs are those which are actively engaged in acquiring, managing, renovating and selling real estate. This is the most profitable types of REITs as a rule, which makes the most common REIT and the most successful. Equity REITs typically focus on a specific type of real estate including resorts and hotels, storage facilities, health care facilities, office facilities, industrial facilities, retail facilities or residential facilities, all of which have different strengths and weaknesses depending on local markets.

As such, if you are planning on investing in one of these types of REITs it is best to do some homework beforehand and determine just what the market is like for the type of real estate in question:

Residential: One of the most common types of REITs is the residential variety that typically deals in condominiums and apartment buildings. You will know if this type of REIT is a good investment if the amount of demand exceeds the supply. If there are lots of new apartment buildings in the area of the REIT's holdings, it might be better to keep looking at additional options.

Retail: REITs that focus on retail are typically further specialized into either shopping malls or shopping centers. The types of properties that these REITs focus on are quite expensive to build which means there will rarely be more space available than the demand calls for. Nevertheless, it is easy to see how successful these REITs are doing, simply visit their holdings and determine for yourself if the complexes or shopping malls are in a period of boom or bust.

Offices and industrial parks: This type of possible REIT candidates are typically subject to longer lease periods which means their profitability is largely tied to how the market was doing when the space was initially rented last. This can go either way for the REIT as a period of low rents can curtail profits for years to come while higher rents will keep things looking up despite the occasional vacancy. To determine what part of the cycle the holdings in question are in you can call properties in the area and check rental rates against long term averages.

Storage: When it comes to jumping on the REIT bandwagon, there is no cheaper way to do so than via a REIT that focuses on storage units. Storage unit use has been rising steadily in the United States for the past 20 years and this type of REIT has proven itself to be reliable and quite resistant to downturns as well. As long as there are not too many competing services in a given area, this type of REIT is almost always going to generate slow and steady profits.

Hotels and resorts: Investing in these REITs is typically on the high end of the cost spectrum and is often one of the riskier propositions as it is closely tied to the general success of the worldwide markets because people simply take fewer vacations when the economy is weak. As such, if you are planning in investing in this type of REIT you will need to be fairly confident in the market in general.

Non-equity REITs

Mortgage REITs: These types of REITs are those that are instead interested in holding, acquiring and underwriting the debt associated with real estate purchases. Buying shares in these REITs are closer to owning a debt portfolio than owning a portion of a physical asset.

Hybrid REITs: For those who simply cannot make up their minds, a hybrid REIT offers investment opportunities for both mortgage loan and equity property investment. While not as common as regular equity REITs, they are a good choice for those looking to diversify as much as possible all in one place.

REIT tips to keep in mind

- Your investment in a REIT is liquid versus other real estate deals.
- You need to assess the growth in earnings, which is made from high occupancy and increasing rents, as well as assess the lower costs and potential new business opportunities.
- Research the management team because it is the team that will decide if a facility is upgraded if more facilities/services are offered, and help to increase the demand for the property.
- You do need to be cautious about wage growth. Wage growth directly effects whether rent can increase. Rent increases can reduce potential renters, even make it impossible for renters to stay in the property they have been renting for years. There is a fine line between increasing rent to make a higher profit and ensuring that the property stays rented. The management team has to know the best option in the rental market to ensure they do not turn away potential income for a thought of gaining higher earnings.

Conclusion

Thanks for making it through to the end of *Real Estate Investing: How To Make Your Riches From Rental Properties and Flipping Houses, And Build Passive Income By Mastering The Property Investment Game*, let's hope it was informative and able to provide you with all of the tools you need to achieve your goals, whatever it is that they may be. Just because you've finished this book doesn't mean there is nothing left to learn on the topic, and expanding your horizons is the only way to find the mastery you seek.

While, generally speaking, the steps to success with real estate investment are relatively straightforward, it is important to not get ahead of yourself early on in the process. While eventually, you will have the network of contacts, leads on upcoming properties and experience finding the best deals, that all comes with time and it is important to manage your expectations accordingly. While it is certainly important to set goals if you hope to be successful in real estate, it is also important that those goals are realistic if you want them to motivate you towards success as opposed to holding you back with unrealistic demands.

All told it may take several months before you have done enough research to find the perfect neighborhood and then several months more before you find the perfect property. While your individual time to profit might be shorter, it is important to keep in mind how long the process might realistically take so that you can be prepared. Just remember, investing in real estate is a marathon, not a sprint which means that slow and steady wins the race.

Finally, if you found this book useful in anyway, a review on Amazon is always appreciated!

Description

Regardless if you are looking to start investing for the first time or are looking to enhance an existing investment portfolio, real estate is an ideal choice. Ideal, that is, if you choose wisely, but the complex ins and outs of the various types of real estate investment make doing so far from a sure thing. If you are interested in ensuring you make the right decisions, then *Real Estate Investing: How To Make Your Riches From Rental Properties and Flipping Houses, And Build Passive Income By Mastering The Property Investment Game* is the book you have been waitin gfor.

Inside you will find everything you need in order to help make the process more straight forward, started with real estate investment successfully starting with the basics including useful investment lingo, how to decide if real estate if real estate is right for you and additional starter tips to help you get started on the right foot. Next, you will learn essentials when it comes to paying for property, finding the ideal property and negotiating the deal when the time comes.

From there you will learn about a wide variety of different real estate investment opportunities including rental property of the traditional and turn key variety as well as the responsibilities that come with being a landlord. You will then learn the ins and out of property flipping including determining when a property is a good deal and building a fix and flip team. Finally, you will learn the basics of property wholesaling and REITs as well.

So, what are you waiting for? Take control of your financial future like never before and buy this book today!

Rental Property Investing:

How to Build and Manage Your Real Estate Empire as well as Creating Passive Income with Rental Properties

By Brandon Anderson

Table of Contents

Introduction

Congratulations on downloading Rental Property Investing and thank you for doing so.

The following chapters will discuss everything that you need to know to begin with this kind of investment opportunity. You can choose from many other investments. You can choose for the stock market, flipping homes, starting a business, helping others put up one, or growing your personal retirement account. But none of them provides you with such unique opportunities and as much potential profit without all the volatility and risk as rental properties.

This guidebook will spend some time looking at rental properties and how you can start this kind of investment on your own. We will look at some of the basics and why this is a great option for an investor, some of the risks you may face, why you need some important people on your team and the different types of properties where you can invest in.

From here, we will move on to some of the steps that you need to get a property and to start the investment. First, we will explore how you can get the financing to buy that property before moving on to the steps of purchasing it, selecting the right tenants, working to maintain and renovate it, and even how to exit the investment when you decide it is time.

Rental property investing is not for everyone. Some people find it as too much work as a landlord and to keep up with demands of a rental property while they take care of their own job and home as well. But for those who want to build up their own empire and are not scared to get to work, rental property is the best investment choice out there. This guidebook will provide you with all the tools that you need to get started with this investment and see some results.

There are plenty of books on this subject on the market. Thanks again for choosing this one! Every effort was made to ensure it is full of as much useful information as possible. Please enjoy!

Chapter 1: Why Rental Properties are the Best Investment Opportunity for You

You can go with many different investment options. Many people like to put their money in the stock market because many companies are investing in it, there are many different strategies they can use while others prefer mutual funds because of its simple yet flexible investment strategies, and it has less management cost. Some people like to start their own businesses and make a living from that. In addition, others will just put their money away in a retirement plan and hope that it is enough to get them by.

However, one of the best ways that you can invest your money is through real estate investing and there are few different methods you can use to do this. It is not easy being a landlord because of the risks involved, the obligations to fulfill, and the requirements that you need to comply. In addition, being a landlord has a lot of advantages: you will be able to receive a decent amount of money per month from the rental properties; you are financially secured as long as there is a tenant; and, since you are the boss, you get to decide on the terms and agreement and when to sell it. While others think that investing in the stock market is much better because the return of investment is superficial (stocks can often make up to 10% while real estate only rises about 3% a year), rental properties still have a lot of benefits. You don't have to start big in this kind of investment; you can start with one property.

Let's see why real estate investment is the best compared to some of the other forms of investment you can choose.

Get Some Great Tax Breaks

There are reasons you would want to consider purchasing a rental property. The first benefit is that the government will offer you some great tax advantages when you do this so that they can get more investors to purchase a rental property, which then causes the supply of rental homes to increase.

You are considered a business owner or an investor under tax laws when you own a rental property. This is good news for you because it lets you make use of more tax deductions and much more benefits, compared to being an average homeowner. For example, you can deduct travelling expenses and property depreciation to help lower your annual taxes. There are many tax benefits available for someone investing in rental properties, and talking with your accountant or financial advisor can ensure that you take advantage of all of them.

Use the Money from the Bank to Fund This Investment

Another reason you should consider purchasing a rental property is you can use other people's money to help pay for it. This is leverage and it can help you to multiply the gains on your property value all at the same time.

Suppose you purchased a rental property for $100,000 and you put down 20% out of your own pocket and the 80% came from the bank. If the property value ends up rising to $110,000, you reaped a return of 50%! However, if you used your own money to fund that same property, then your returns are only 10%. 10% is still fine, but not as profitable as the 50%.

Most lenders will finance between 50-80% of the property price as long as you can come up with down payment and have a good credit history. In addition, finance companies are another place to look for a loan for a rental property.

The Rental Property Can be Used as an Asset to Secure More Loans in the Future

At first, you may wonder why a rental property is considered an asset by a bank or another financial institute. It is important because once you have paid off a touch of the mortgage for your rental property; you can then use this as collateral.

What does this mean? You can pledge your rental property as an asset to get another loan if you need. This is helpful if you want to purchase another rental property down the road or if you want to start a new business later.

By paying off your monthly mortgage—through the rental payment of tenants—you can not only build up equity but also your personal credit scores. When you have a high credit score, you will have a higher chance of loan approval and lower interest rates next time that you want to take a loan out.

Losses for Your Rental Properties Can Be Covered by Some Tax Relief

Besides all the tax deductions that we discussed earlier, investing in a rental property can also bring some tax relief if you end up with some losses. At first, some of your rental expenses may be high and they could exceed the rent you receive from your tenants. Expenses such as utility bills, repair costs, property insurance, and mortgage payment can easily take over your income at first. This can make it so that you make a loss in the beginning.

While these losses are not something that you want to see with an investment, the silver lining in all of these is rental losses can be used as a tax deduction against your other taxable income. Of course, this isn't the sole reason for you investing in a rental property, but it can help if it becomes tough for the first few years. As you pay off the mortgage and fix up the home, and as market values increase so you can raise rental payments, you will start to see a profit from this work.

Values in Property Are Usually Less Volatile Than the Stock Market

Stocks can be a great investment, ones that can be bought and sold as quickly and as easily as you would like. This is good for someone who wants to try out the stock market, but then discovers it's not for them and they want out immediately. But because of this, stock prices can fluctuate much more than rental property values. In fact, a stock price can be so volatile that it could move up and down 5% or more in one day.

Real estate is more of a long-term investment. That is why the property market–while it goes up in most areas–is not that volatile. When you purchase a property to use as a rental investment, you don't plan to take it and sell it within a few weeks or even a few months. You plan to keep it for many years so you can pay down the mortgage and earn money. And most people who get into the market of real estate outside of flippers–who are rare and far between– plan to purchase a home and stick with it for a long time.

This can help keep the market for housing more stable. When you purchase a property, you won't have to worry about it going up or down in value in a short period of time. This means buying and selling a property can take more time. But this really stabilizes real estate prices, which can help shield your investment from overnight market crashes and other sell outs that happen in the stock market.

Can Create a Passive Income for You

Your rental income can be more stable and frequent compared to some of the cash flow that you get from other investments. Your tenants–as long as you keep the property filled–will pay you the monthly rent, allowing you to have a stream of cash flow as long as you pay the monthly mortgage and taxes on the property on time.

Most rental property owners receive some rent from their tenants every month. However, if you're going with the stock market, your bonds would only pay you some interest every six months and stocks will only pay dividends every year, and that only happens if the company actually makes a profit.

Another reason rental properties may be the best option to go with is that if you hire a property manager to handle the day-to-day activities, then this becomes a hands-free affair and you are effectively earning a passive income from your work.

Rental properties have many benefits that you can enjoy. They take a touch of workin the beginning to get up and running, and they require maintenance and finding the right tenants. But if you can get all of these organized, you will quickly see that they are perfect for helping you get a steady cash flow; they can give you tax breaks and can even provide you with equity that can be used on future loans.

Chapter 2: What Are Some of the Risks with Rental Properties?

Like any other type of investment, there are a lot of advantages when you own a rental property. However, there are also some risks involved when it comes to purchasing a rental property. You have to remember: this is a business endeavor and not just something fun to do on the side. A lot of money goes into rental properties–you are purchasing a whole house–and you have to be prepared for this new investment so you can make the most money possible. This chapter is going to focus on some of the risks that can come up with rental properties and some of the things you can do to limit these risks and get the best results.

Buying a Property That Is in Worse Condition Than You Expected

The first thing you need to do when you get into this investment is pick the right property. You want the right location, the right price, and a property that won't take too long or won't cost too much to fix up. When you are looking for an investment property, you need to think of it as a business rather than a personal home that you will live in. You want a property that will make a good profit for you as soon as possible. You don't want to get reckless and overspend on the property before the first tenant walks in the door.

To help you avoid the risk of purchasing a new property that is in worse shape than expected, ensure that you get an inspection done. You need to bring an inspector to the property with you before purchasing. This takes up a few hours of your time, but these professionals will discover any problems or hidden damages that should be fixed before you rent out the property. They will also give you some ideas on spending budget to update the property before you purchase.

Not Being Able to Get a Tenant for a Long Period of Time

Another risk is not being able to get tenants. Once you purchase a good property and once it is ready to be rented out, you may run into trouble finding tenants. This is even riskier if you took a loan out from a bank to help purchase the property and you expected to get some rent each month to cover those payments. If you end up not being able to find the right tenant, you should cover up the mortgage, the property taxes, the insurance, and other expenses from your own salary or savings.

Look for tenants immediately, even before you finish purchasing the property. This gives you some leeway time to find the right tenants and you will get them inthe right time when the property is ready. You don't want to choose the first tenants that come along because this can cost you more money than not having a one. By starting early, you give yourself some room to find the right people to rent from you.

You can reduce this risk by doing your research and choosing a good property to invest in. Choose a property that is in a high-demand location with high-occupancy rates. The more in-demand your property is, the easier it is to get tenants.

Having Bad Tenants

While finding some tenants to live in your rental properties is important so you can make money, there are times you can't be provided with a profit. This happens when you end up choosing a bad tenant. Having that kind of tenant and not evicting them can sometimes be even worse than the risk of not having anyone to start with. Yes, no tenant means no earning; but with that kind of tenant, they may not pay the rent, they may destroy the house, and they may end up costing you more time and money than not having one.

Each property can become damaged a bit simply from people living in it. But bad tenants take this to the next level and may destroy things. They may refuse to pay your rent for a few months, making your cash flow stop. You then have to file a notice to a local court, schedule the date, and show up there, empty out the property, and then do the repairs before you can get a new tenant. These evictions can be costly and take a long time. You are spending on the mortgage and other expenses without earning any profits in the process.

It is best if you can avoid this risk to start with. Have some high selection criteria before you pick a tenant. You can write out your tenant rules ahead of time. You don't want to discriminate against someone for their social status, religion, gender, or age because this can get you in legal trouble. But you can look at their credit score, some references, and their past rental history to help you make informed decisions. This may make it so you will have vacant periods, but you will be further ahead doing this than being more costly for having a bad tenant.

The Expenses on the Property Are Higher Than You Anticipated

When you become a landlord, the potential costs will not end just because you purchased the property. These rental properties will require constant expenses. You have to pay the mortgage payment, taxes (often higher a primary home tax), insurance, maintenance (varies depending on the type of tenants you have), and more.

If you calculated the right way and priced the rent well, then income that you make from your tenants will cover these expenses. Hopefully, you can also earn a positive cash flow from what's left. That is your overall goal when you start investing in rental properties.

But at times, the expenses may end up being more than what was anticipated. Maybe a tenant comes and causes a mess throughout the house. Maybe something major breaks and you have to fix it. Or, the market could go down and you aren't able to charge as much rent as you need.

Having a plan in place is very important before you even consider venturing this type of investment.

To avoid any risks of paying more for the rental property rather than making money off it, ensure you really do your homework before you become a landlord. Get a pen and some paper and do the math. Make the correct calculations before you purchase a property so you know how much it will cost and how much you will earn. Add another 5% to give yourself a bit of wiggle room. If you wouldn't get a positive cash flow from this, then you shouldn't purchase the property.

The Real Estate Market Starts to Fall

In recent times, the real estate market has been growing. But while the trend is positive, there really isn't a guarantee that this kind of trend is going to continue. One risk that you may encounter first with rental property investing is the concentration of your assets. For the most part, when you own a rental property, this is a serious concentration of assets because you will spend a larger portion of your net worth—sometimes all of it—just to get the property.

As the landlord, the first property investment is not going to be diversified—you only have one property at this point. If the neighborhood, the city, or even the national economy starts to go down, you could end up losing a large portion of your investment when depreciation occurs.

One option that you can follow to help reduce this risk is to diversify your investment a bit. This is not easy as a beginner because purchasing rental properties is expensive. You aren't selling them and making a profit, so you don't have any money to purchase another. But you can pull your money together with other investors and start a residential investment company. This is basically a small business that buys, rents, and sells rental properties.

Rental properties are a great investment that can help you to earn a great deal of money, especially over a long-term period. The benefits far outweigh the possible risks, but it is still important to understand that there are some risks with this type of investment, just like with any other form of investing. You should be aware of these risks and learn how to avoid them to get the best return on your investment.

Chapter 3: The Best People to Work with During Your Investment

When you venture into rental property investing, you will find that you are not able to do all the work alone. This will just make the work harder than it should be and you will probably give up and not earn. Having a good team behind you the whole time can really make the process go smoothly and can help to reduce some of the risks that you face.

The people you want in your team can vary depending on the work you want to put in and the kind of project you are working on. Your team may include a mentor, a real estate agent, a contractor, and a good loan officer. Let's take a look at each of these individuals and explore why they can be so important in making your investment successful.

Your Family

Working as a rental property investor takes a lot of time and work. You have to learn the market and search around for the right property. You have to make a purchase of that property. You have to do the repairs on the property and find the right tenants to live there. Even when tenants are there, you have to spend time doing any repairs and collecting rent. The work of a landlord can be rewarding, but it takes up a lot of your time and will keep going, even after you purchase the property.

You will need the support of your family during this time. You may need them to help you out with some of the repairs. You may need them to vent to during tough situations. In some cases, your family may be the ones who loan you money to help with purchasing the property or repairing it. There is nothing better for your overall success than having your family to support you through this process.

A Mentor

Getting into real estate can be difficult. There are many things that you have to focus on, including the market status, how much you are spending, and finding tenants to name a few. Learning all those stuff before you get into the market can be a great way to reduce your risks, but nothing beats real-life experience. Working with an experienced mentor, who is willing to talk it over and offer advice when needed, can be an invaluable asset to you.

There are lots of places you can look for a mentor. You can talk to someone who has done real estate flipping or rental properties. These individuals have personal experiences doing the work and they can really show you how the process gets done. Depending on who you work with, they may even let you come along on some of the work and see how the process works upfront.

If you can not make connections with anyone who invests in rental properties in your area, then you can talk to real estate agents, contractors, or other people who work with properties and they can give you some insight into how to do this type of investment.

An Accountant

At first, you may decide that you don't want to work with an accountant. You want to just handle this on your own and not to deal with another person. But even when you are starting and especially further down the line, you may decide that it is worth your time to have an accountant on your side.

A good and reliable accountant can help you keep track of all the finances of your new business. They can help you figure out current rent prices, determine the right price for the home, and help you set up a budget. And, they will help you during tax time to ensure you get the most tax deductions possible. In the long run, your accountant can end up saving you money!

You can explore a few different accountants to see who suits best for your needs. You might consider hiring an experienced accountant who has handled real estate accounts. They can ensure that you are getting your taxes done correctly and they will answer your questions about rental properties.

A Good Loan Officer

As a rental property investor, you will work your way into owning not just one property. And until you really start to build up your equity in your properties or you have enough cash flow to purchase the property outright, you will need a loan to help finance your purchases. You will find that it is easier for you to work with the same loan officer each time. They can answer your questions and they know your payment and credit history. They can even offer new loan products and more to you that will help you get the most out of your investment.

We will talk about your loan officer more in the next chapter, but you need to carefully consider who you want to work with. There are many options. Local banks and credit unions are often best for this kind of investment. They want to help their local economy grow and they often have the best rates. Check into what rates each company can offer, pose questions, and see what requirements that the financial institute needs to help you get a loan.

A Real Estate Agent

As the buyer of a rental property, it is a good idea to work with a real estate agent. The buyer's agent is going to be paid through the seller, which means you can enjoy their services and they will be there for you without you having to spend anything out of your own budget.

A real estate agent can be a valuable resource because they know the area really well. They have some great connections and can find some of the properties for you. Using the MLS and their contacts, you may even be able to hear about properties coming up on the market before anyone else does.

Your agent can be useful during the purchasing as well: they will do the paperwork for you; negotiate for the best price; help you get the inspections done; a good resource for finding workers that you need to do any major or minor fixes in the house. In some cases, they may even be able to recommend some potential tenants to help you get the renting started.

You can certainly choose to purchase a home on your own, but since the agent can provide you with a lot of resources and the seller is the one paying them, it is worth your time to find an agent to work with, at least in the beginning. If you are a beginner and don't know the market well and you don't want to deal with all of the paperwork, then hiring a real estate agent can make a big difference.

A General Contractor

It is a good idea to have a general contractor that you can call when looking at a rental property, even after purchasing. To get the best price on a rental property, you should get a home that needs a little work. If it is brand new or in amazing shape, you are going to find the price is too high for your budget and you won't earn in the process.

Since you are going to work with some fixer-uppers in the process, you will need to work with a general contractor. They can take some time to look through the home before you purchase and help you know whether there are any major or minor fixes that need to be done and how much will be the cost. This can make a difference in whether you actually purchase the property or not, and can save you from some big surprises down the line.

Once you purchase the property, you can also use the general contractor to help you make some of the fixes. With some of the minor jobs, you can do them. But if you don't have the time, or if it is a major job that needs a professional, the contractor can do the work for you. A good general contractor will offer a good price, will complete the work quickly, and can work with you on any project.

Having the right team of professionals on your side can make the rental investment process easier. They can support you, help you keep track of all the finances, help you find a property, and even help you get the financing that you need to get you started. Take your time to find the right people to join your team and get the best results.

Chapter 4: The Best Types of Rental Properties You Can Purchase and Make Money From

When you are ready to invest in rental properties, there are actually a few different options that you can choose from. Some are going to earn you more potential profits, but you should put in more work than others. Some will earn less profit in the beginning, but the tenants usually do a better job maintaining it and they will stay around. You have to balance the benefits and the risks of each option and decide which one is the best for you. Some of the different rental properties that you can choose from for your investment include:

Apartments

The first option we are going to look at is apartments. These often include quite a few living arrangements in one building and can have a lot of potential for profits depending on how many rooms you can keep full with tenants. If you have 100 units in the building, there can be a large amount of profit with a reasonable rent. When renting these out, you should consider the rental charges, the allowed number of tenants in each unit, and whether or not you will take care of the utilities cost in the rent. You will be responsible for maintenance like mowing the grass and snow removal throughout the year.

However, there are some disadvantages. Yes, you can make a lot of income, but keeping an apartment up and running can take a lot of work. And each of those tenants will have problems that they want you to fix. Apartments are also notoriously known for high turnover rates. Being able to keep all the units occupied at all times can be almost impossible and you may spend a lot of time advertising for and screening potential tenants to keep your income stream coming in throughout the year.

Duplexes

Duplexes are the best of both worlds, combining the extra profits from apartments with some of the ease of a single-family home. These properties will usually have between two to eight separate living arrangements or apartments available, so you can open it up and split the mortgage payment between many people. You will have more work than you would find with a single-family home, but the potential income is much higher. Many tenants who go to duplexes are going to be around a lot longer than you find with an apartment, which can provide a good stream of income without having to search for new ones all the time.

Another benefit of these properties is that you can also live in one of them. If your property has eight living spots, you could rent out seven of them and let those tenants pay for the mortgage on their own. This gives you free living arrangements—the tenants pay for it for you—and you can just one call away if something happens that you need to take care of.

Single-Family Homes

A lot of investors like to go with a single-family home to help them make an income from their property. These properties are easy to manage and often, the family that agrees to be your tenant will stay around for a couple years. They want to have stability and they don't like to move around for a long time. If you can get them in, you can have a steady income for a long time.

The downside to these types of properties is that they can only hold one family at a time so you won't be able to make a larger income like you can with apartments and duplexes. But most tenants who move into these homes will take good care of them and it will be less work on your side.

Commercial Real Estate

You also have the option to rent out commercial real estate. This allows you to rent out office building, commercial spaces, or storefronts to interested businesses or companies. This takes more initial capital to get started, but it can definitely be worth it to make a large income.

There are many different types of properties that can fit here: you could own a single store or a strip mall and rent out to a lot of different tenants. If you own a spacious warehouse, you may rent it out to a company. You have to decide what kind of risk and investment you want to start with and which one works with your investing style.

There are some benefits to working with this. First, you can charge a higher rent so the potential for profit is higher. And, most businesses are interested in staying around for a long time because this provides more stability to their customers. This can provide you with a really steady income for three or more years. You may want to consider offering them a discount on the rent if they agree to stay for a longer period of time.
There are some disadvantages to this kind of investment as well, though. This investment type charges more upfront costs than some of the other options. This can make it harder to get into when you are starting and you may have to wait until you can save up more money to make it happen. Also, if one of your tenants or businesses ends up moving out, it can be hard to find someone to replace them and you would have to handle the mortgage and other expenses on your own.

These are just a few of the different properties that you will need to consider when you want to get into this kind of investing. There are some benefits and risks to each one, so you need to consider each of them and see which one seems the best for you.

Chapter 5: Getting the Right Financing to Start Your Business and Help It Grow

When you are looking for a property to use as an investment, you also need to consider how you will finance it. It is unlikely that you will already have enough money to pay for it out of the pocket, so you will need to find some other methods to do it. Here, we are going to explore the available options that can help you finance the rental property so you can purchase it and start making money.

Get a Conventional Loan from the Bank

Most rental property investors choose to go with a conventional bank loan. These often have the best terms and offer the most security when it comes to financing your investment property. If you own a residence, then you already have an idea of how to work with conventional financing.

A conventional mortgage conforms to the guidelines that Freddie Mac and Fannie Mae set up. And unlike some of the other loan options, like a USDA, VA, or FHA loan, it is not backed up by the federal government. With this conventional mortgage, you will need to put a 20% down payment on the home. Since this is more of an investment than a personal purchase, you may need to provide up to 30% for the down payment. You could use gifted funds to help pay this down payment, but you must make sure you document it properly before getting the mortgage.

When you work with a conventional loan, your personal credit score and history will be used to help determine if you will get approved and what interest rate you will get on the mortgage. These lenders are also going to take a look at your assets and income and the borrowers should be able to afford their current bills as well as the loan payments on the new property. Even if you plan to have a rent covering the rental property, you should be able to pay these out of pocket if things don't go well.

Do a Hard Money Loan

One option that you should go with is a hard money loan. These loans can work for some investors because they are short-term loans that are not given out by a bank. Sure, you want to keep the property for long-term and may not be able to make the large payments for a long time and make a profit. But if you find that getting conventional funding is just not working for you, this option can help build up your credit score and you can get a conventional mortgage down the road.

This kind of loan can be useful because it looks more at the value of the property you want to purchase rather than on your personal credit. A good investor may go with this loan and while it works best with a property flip, it can help you get started.

When you know exactly what you want to get with your property, you can add in some higher than average loan costs to this formula. But make sure that you will not get into a lot of debt when you use this. This is riskier because the payments each month will be much larger. You want to go with a hard money loan, one that is beneficial to you and doesn't have too high of payments, and one that you will be able to convert over to a conventional loan later on to save you money.

Working with a hard money loan can be really expensive and you need to factor these expenses into your profitability calculations. These lenders will charge a very high interest rate—usually at least 14%—and they can carry multiple points and have high closing costs. Points are going to be paid up-front with each point being about 1% of the loan amount. This can cost you more upfront, but it helps when you need a quick short-term loan to finance the investment.

Do a Fix and Flip loan

While being a landlord has a lot of perks, there are times when it will be a headache for the investor. You may decide that flipping is a better option. it means re-selling the property in order to make a big lump sum of money in the process.

These loans are often a smaller term and can be easier to get compared to a full 30-year mortgage. You have to work hard to get the property up and running and ready to sell to make the most profit. You can make a lot of money from this, but you also have to consider that you aren't earning any equity in the property and you won't be able to enjoy a steady stream of income when you choose this option.

If you are having trouble getting a loan to help you with this project, it may be a good idea to consider a short-term loan. This can help you get some of the financing that you need and can build up your credit history in the process. The monthly payments will be larger, but after a bit, you may be able to switch down to a less expensive option and the amount of equity that you earn in the process will be higher.

Find a Local Investor in the Area

If some of the other options for financing do not work for you, then you may look for an investor who would help you out. You can start by searching in your local community. This can be tricky, though, because individual investors want to find ways to protect themselves so that you can't just run off with their money. But they may be excited to get started with the investment and may provide you with better rates than other options.

Choosing this option can be a great way to earn the financing you need at good rates. Before you approach an investor, make sure that you have a plan in place to impress them. Show them your investment plans, answer their questions, and even show them the terms that you are interested in sharing with them if they invest their money with you.

Owner Financing

You should also consider doing owner financing on the property. There are some owners who are willing to do this kind of financing. They find that it earns them extra on the sale of their home and opens up the market to more buyers than waiting for someone with a conventional mortgage. You can get what you want without going through a traditional bank, and the seller can make even more money on their house.

For this option–instead of working to get a conventional mortgage–you would instead make monthly payments to the person who owns the property now. You would have to come up with a down payment at the time that you close, but this is often less than 10%. The owner will be charged with the interest as well, setting it about 1 or 2 percentage points above the conventional mortgage rates, but sometimes they may consider setting it higher. When you are ready to resell the property, you will pay off the remainder of the loan balance and you can keep the profit.

Many investors will try to look for this kind of option if they want to purchase a property, but they can't come up with a good down payment to use traditional methods. The owner is just going to carry the mortgage for that property, using the method they did to purchase it. You would still pay for the repairs and take ownership of the property. The hardest part is often finding the right seller who would do this.

Another option similar to this is using an owner financing. This is when you purchase the property as "subject to" the ongoing mortgage. The buyer will pay the seller the amount between the purchase price and the balance left on the mortgage at that time. They then take over the payments of the seller's mortgage. However, you need to double-check before you decide to do this because some mortgage contracts say this is not allowable.

Tap into Your Home Equity
Another option that you can work with is to draw on the equity in your personal residence. You can do this through a home equity loan or through a cash-out refinance. Depending on your mortgage and the rules in your area, you can borrow up to 80% of the equity value of your home towards purchasing a second home. If you have paid off quite a bit of your personal home and have some equity, this could be a great way to get the money that you need for this investment.

There are some benefits and risks in using this kind of financing, and often, it depends on the loan type that you go with. With a home equity loan, you are going to borrow against the equity of your home in a similar way that you would with a credit card. And for a specific amount of time, the payments would just be on the interest. The rate on this is variable, which means there is the potential it will go up if the prime rate rises.

You can also go with a cash-out refinance. This option has a fixed rate, but often it extends the life of the mortgage you already have. This longer term for the loan means that you pay more in interest over the life of the mortgage on the primary residence. You would need to weigh this against the expected returns that your investment property will bring in.

Tips to Help You Get the Financing You Need for Your Investment

In addition to following some of the steps above, there are a few other things that you can do to increase your chances of getting the financing that your new investment needs. Some of the best tips that you can get financing include:

- *A good down payment*: Since your mortgage insurance isn't going to cover properties used for investing, you should put down a minimum of 20% to help secure the traditional financing that you want. If you can put down 25% or more down, you may be able to get an even better rate for your property. If you are looking at rental properties and you don't have the down payment, it may be time to look at other options. You can consider a second mortgage for that property, but that is difficult to get.

- *Being a borrower the banks like*: There are a lot of factors that come into play when the bank or other financial institution decides to give you a loan. One thing that you can do ahead of time is to check your credit score and see you can improve to make it better. If it is below 740, it will cost you more money to get the same interest rate on your score. Also, make sure that you have enough money in the bank to cover six months of living expenses because this can make you look more attractive to a bank.

- *Stay away from the big banks*: Big banks are all about the bottom line and if you have anything on your history that is less than stellar, they will either deny you the loan or charge outrageous rates so you have a hard time making a profit at all. Local banks and credit unions are much better options. They will take more diverse customers than the big banks and they want to see their local community grow. If you have any blemishes on your credit or you want to work with someone who is a bit easier, then working with a local financial institution can be better.

- *Considering owner financing*: This is hard to come by in some cases, but there are some times you may be able to get the owner to do the financing for you. You may have to convince the seller to do this for you because they don't want to keep the property and they don't want their credit score ruined in the process. You should come up with a contract and stick with the agreements to make this work.

- *Thinking creatively*: If you are looking at a good property and you think it will do well with investing, you may want to find some creative methods to get the down payment or even the money to do renovations. Using credit cards, insurance policies, or a home equity line of credit can help you out here. Be careful and weigh whether these options are good and if you can to pay them back. For example, credit cards contain high-interest rates so you should be careful in using them.

Financing an investment property can take some time. Lenders want to make sure that you have a good credit score; that you have a good plan behind your investment. They also want to make sure that you can afford your current bills and the new loan amount that you are asking for. Work with some of the tips above and you will find that it is easier than you think to get the funding that your investment property needs.

Steps to Help You Get the Funding That You Want

When you are ready to get the financing, it is important to know the steps in order to get funding for your loan. The first step is to check out your credit score. All financial institutions are going to take a look at your credit score to make sure that you don't have too much debt, that you don't have any late payments, and that there is nothing else that they need to be concerned about when they give you a loan.

If you take a look at your credit score and notice that there is something that may concern them, or you see that your score is not high enough, then you should work on it before you try to reach out to a financial institution. Get some of your debts paid down, find out how you can close out some bad accounts, and learn other ways that you can put up with your credit score so you look more attractive to a lender.

Next, you need to write out a business plan to show to the financial institution. This is not just a loan for your personal home. It is to help you start out a new investment and a new business. This means you need to treat it that way. The financial institution who becomes your lender will also want to see that you have a plan in place and that you have an entry strategy, a reasonable timeline, enough money to pay off the mortgage while you wait for a tenant, and that you have a good exit strategy in place.

Take the time to write this business plan out and make it look professional and well-thought-out. You can find some templates to help with this so you can really impress the lender. You should show this to every lender you want to work with, so keep a few extra copies on hand to make it easier when you need to talk to a new lender.

You should also have a down payment. This is a loan for an investment so you are not going to get some of the other options such as no down payment like you can with a personal home loan. You should come up with some form of down payment, and the larger this payment can be, the better off you will be. You can discuss the best amount with your lender. A larger amount will not only give you more equity in the property but can also save you a lot of money since you can get a lower interest rate.

You may need to show some other information as well. If you have ever purchased a home for your personal use, then you know a lot of what the lender is going to look for. You need your pay stubs and that of anyone who is going to be on the loan with you such as your spouse or a partner, information about any debts, and more. If the bank asks for anything else, make sure to get this information to them as quickly as possible. This can help speed up the process and will get your loan money in your pocket as quickly as possible.

Make sure that you take the time to shop around. Even local banks in the same town can offer you different rates and benefits for working with them. If you shop around and compare the rates and offers from several banks—at least two or three—you will ensure that you are getting the best deal and won't have to pay any more on the loan than necessary.

After you have presented this information to a few lenders, you should start to get some offers, as long as all the information is in place. Then you can compare the offers that you get and pick the one that will help cover the loan at the lowest rates. The lower rate is going to make a difference in how much you are going to spend over the life of the loan, as well as how much the payment will be every month. Carefully look over each one to make sure you get the best deal possible when you sign.

Chapter 6: What Makes a Good Rental Property?

Now that you have some ideas of where to get your financing and you are now ready to start searching around, you may wonder what is going to make a good property to help you get started with investing in rental properties. There are several different factors to help you analyze all of the properties that you look for. It is best to consider each of them to ensure you are getting the best property that will earn the most money. Some of the things that you should consider when picking out a good rental property to invest in will include the following:

The Neighborhood

The quality of the neighborhood you purchase in is going to influence your vacancy rate and the tenants you will get. For example, if you purchase a property that is near a college, your tenants will be mostly students, and you will have vacancies on a regular basis such as during the summer breaks and when a semester ends.

Knowing your target market can really make it easier for you to pick out the right neighborhood. You can think about what your perfect tenant is looking for when they rent, and then look in that neighborhood so you can provide it to them. Each type of tenant prefers a different area. For example, a family will want an area near the schools and parks and with other children but an older couple may want to be somewhere quieter.

In addition, check out the rules in some neighborhoods. There are some municipalities that don't want to see the homes turned into rentals so they will put up a lot of red tapes and high permit fees to help discourage this kind of investing.

How Much the Property Costs

When looking at properties, you need to consider how much it costs. You don't want to go for an expensive property. If so, the mortgage, insurance, and taxes are going to be too much and you won't be able to charge enough in rent to cover all of it.

You always have to look for properties that are lower in price but won't need a lot of money on the renovations. Before purchasing the property, you should get a calculator and figure out the numbers. Look at how much the mortgage will be and how high the interest is. Look at how much you will spend each month on any repairs, the taxes, insurance, and everything else you owe on the property. Also, include a little bit so you can earn a profit.

Take that number and compare it to the average rent in your area. If it is at or under this number, then the property is perfect for you and you should consider putting in a bid. If the amount ends up being lower than the average rent, you can raise it and make an even larger profit in the process. Never invest in a property without running all the numbers ahead of time.

How Much Work Needs to Be Done

You also need to consider how much work the property needs to have done. If you purchase a property for a good price, but then you have to completely remodel it, this is going to take more time and money than you can afford. You should spend a little bit on renovations when it comes to purchasing a rental property, you don't want to spend too much of your budget on this part.

As you look through properties, take notes and some pictures. You can even consider bringing a contractor along with you to look over the property. This gives you a good idea of how much work you should do, and then you can get estimates on how much it will cost. If you can purchase the property and fix it up while still making a profit on the rent you would charge, then this property is a good one to invest in.

Property Taxes

The next thing that you need to take a look at when checking out a property is its taxes. You will quickly find that when you look at a town, the property taxes are not the same in all areas. If the area is newer–if you are near schools and if you are closer to the country–you may pay a different property tax than anyone else. You need to know exactly the property taxes that will be charged to you.

You need to know the exact amount of property taxes ahead of time. If you wait until after the property is yours, you may be in for a bit of sticker shock. Don't try to come up with an estimate on this either. Some investors will look at other similar properties and try to guess their property taxes. But each property is different and depending on its size, where it is located, how big and more, the property taxes may be different than other similar properties. Visit the country assessor in your area to get an accurate number for this one.

Schools

If you are purchasing a home big enough for a family, then you also need to take a look at some of the local educational facilities nearby. If a property is good but the schools are not close by, then it is going to greatly affect the value of your investment. While you have some concerns about the cash flow you will get each month, the overall value of the rental property is going to come into play when you sell it, and having a property near schools can make a big difference.

If you are in a market that has several options for schools, consider which the best is. You should need to pick out a property that is near a private school to help attract those properties. Or if you know one of the schools doesn't do well with state testing, you should need to avoid that one when you pick out your property.

Crime Rate

No one wants to move somewhere that has a lot of criminal activity or a high crime rate. Even when they are renting rather than buying, they want to make sure they live in a place that is safe and secure for them and their families. You can choose at your local library or check with the police in order to see the crime statistics in all the neighborhoods near you. Some of the concerns that you need to pay particular attention to include vandalism, petty crimes, serious crimes, and how recent the activity of crime is. You can also ask how frequently the police get called to the area to help see if it is a safe option for you to invest in and if your tenants will like it.

If you are uncertain about how the crime rate is in one area, make sure to find out. You can talk to the local police to help you with this. They can answer all your questions and will give you more information than you can find from anywhere else. You can also make an inquiry around town to see if there are any areas that might be noisy or might have other issues that you should be aware of before making a purchase.

Job Market

You need to look at the employment rates in the area you are considering purchasing. If the job market is poor, then it is hard to find tenants who can pay higher rates. You should find a location that has growing employment opportunities because these are going to attract more people to the area, which means that you have more potential tenants.

To help you figure out the employment rates in a particular area, just head to the local library or to the U.S. Bureau of Labor Statistics. If you notice in the newspaper that there is a new company moving to your area or nearby, then this may be a good place to invest in before all the workers flock to the area.

Now, it is possible that the housing prices are not going to move the way that you want. For example, the housing prices are going to react, either in a positive or a negative way, depending on the company moving in. The fallback point here is that if you want to move to the town that has this company, then your renters will like this area as well. If they wouldn't be happy with that company, you probably shouldn't invest here.

Amenities

Take the time to check out the potential neighborhood for current or projected public transport hubs, theaters, gyms, hospitals, malls, parks, and other perks that renters might be interested in. Cities—and even specific parts of a city—have a lot of promotional literature that can inform what public amenities are available. You can then look at an area that has a lot of amenities and see if there are some reasonable properties that will meet your needs for a rental investment property.

The amenities that are the most important will vary depending on what kind of tenant you are looking to work with. If you are interested in working with college kids, you will want to have the college nearby or some local restaurants and night spots. If you are catering to single professionals, you want to make sure you are near the business district. If you are catering to families, then you want to make sure that parks, schools, and other family-friendly activities are nearby.

Future Development in That Area

You also need to take a look at whether or not there will be any future developments in that area. The municipal planning department can provide you with all the information you need about the new developments that will happen in thearea or even any that is currently zoned in that area.

If you look through this information and you notice there are new business parks, malls, and apartment buildings going up in this area, this is a good thing because it shows this is a good growth area. While this growth can be important, you need to watch out for it a little bit. Sometimes a new development could harm the price of the properties nearby, such as when they cause the loss of activity-friendly green space in a family-friendly area. This additional new housing may also provide some competition for your property, which can make it harder to get tenants.

Number of Vacancies and Listings in That Area

If you are looking through the market and you notice that one area or neighborhood has a very large number of listings, then this is something that you can look into. You may see that it is a seasonal cycle and will end soon, or it is a sign that the neighborhood has gone bad. As an investor, you need to figure out which is happening before you purchase. If the neighborhood has gone bad, it is probably not a good idea for you to purchase a home there because you will not find any tenants.

Similar to the idea of listing, the vacancy rates in a particular neighborhood will help you know whether you will have success in attracting tenants. A high rate in vacancies means that you should have lower than average rents in order to attract tenants. Low vacancies can be good for you as a landlord because it means you can raise the rental rates.

How High the Rent Is

When you purchase this type of investment, you are planning on earning money from the rent that your tenants pay. You need to know the average rent in the area so you can base your own rental prices from the property you want to purchase. If you look at the average rent and find that you can't be able to cover the mortgage, taxes, insurance, and repairs of a property, then you should keep looking. You should never go into the investment assuming that you can charge way more than the average price for a property because tenants will not agree to rent from you.

You can research the area well enough so you can also gauge where the rents will go in the next five years. If you can afford the area at this time, but you find that there are some big improvements that need to be done and the property taxes will soon increase, the amount you spend may get too high and you won't be able to afford it later.

Basically, you need to do the math and if you can get the property and pay all the expenses while making a bit of an income while staying at market rent prices, then this is a good investment. If you are worried about doing this, then you should consider a different property to help you earn an income.

if you are finding this book useful in any way, a review on Amazon is always appreciated!

Always overestimate rather than underestimate when it comes to this. You don't want to purchase the property, fix it up, and then search for some tenants just to find out that you are not able to charge the amount of rent you wanted for that property. It is always best to add another 5 to 10% to your costs to make sure you get everything covered.

Natural Disasters

Preparedness is the key during a natural disaster. You will never know when an earthquake, tornado, or hurricane will strike or a flood will rise in your area, whether it is located in a high-risk zone or not.

As a landlord, you should pay attention to the structural details of the property you want to put your money into. It is very important to run a check on the roof, walls, and most especially all the building's foundation. For old buildingsor houses, wear and tearare normal so you need to make sure that it has been reinforced. Before you purchase a property, ensure that, as much as possible, it is at its excellent condition.

You also need to secure an insurance when purchasing a rental property. You need to have a sufficient insurance coverage for the building structure and its contents; you need to also have a firm idea on how much you will spend for insurance on your property so you can factor this into your costs. If you are purchasing a property located in an area prone to tornadoes,hurricanes, flooding, earthquakes, and other natural disasters, you are going to pay extra for this insurance coverage. This can really cut into your profits if you are not cautious. You must do these calculations ahead of time so better if you talk to an insurance provider and seek for the policies they offerand what rates are for the area you want to purchase in.

Choosing the right rental property can make all the difference when it comes to how successful you are. If you pick out a property that is slightly worn out or you have to pay a lot extra in insurance, it could eat away at your profits and can even make it hard to find the right tenants.

Chapter 7: How Do I Purchase My First Property for This Type of Investment

At this point, it is time to start looking at the steps you should take in order to find the first property and then purchase it. This is actually a longer process. It is not as simple as running out and purchasing the first property that gets on the market. When you put money into a property, remember these things: be well-informed about this type of investment and create a winning mindset.

You need to fully understand the market you are working with, get the right financing, find tenants, make an offer, fix up the home, and collect rent money in the process. All of these come together to help you become a good landlord.

Let's take a look at some of the steps that you need to follow in order to purchase your first rental property.

Do Your Research Fully Before Chasing the Property

It is easy as a new investor to jump directly into this and purchase the first property that you find. But you need to do your research before you enter the market. As soon as you decide that rental investing is the right decision for you, you need to do your homework, researching, and learning as much about the market as you can. Some of the questions that you may want to consider to help you with your research include researching:

- What type of property do you want to purchase for this investment?
- How much can you afford and are comfortable with paying?
- What kind of neighborhood are you interested in purchasing and investing in?
- What is the average rent in that area and can you work with that to earn money?
- What is the return on investment you are hoping to make and is that reasonable for that area?

As a beginner, you may find that doing your research can be hard, mainly because you are not yet sure what kind of questions you should ask. Think about this as a new business, because that is what an investment is, and think about all the questions that you should ask before making this important decision.

Decide Who Your Target Market Is

One thing you should consider when you are ready to look for some investment properties is your target market. This may seem somewhat silly, but it can actually really influence the properties you pick and the way that you conduct your business.

Are you looking for a single-family home that a family will move in and stay in for a few years? Then you should consider a nice family home that has three or four bedrooms near the schools, near some parks, near some malls, and where other families with children live. If you want to cater to the older generation, you would want to look for properties that are in safe parts of town, properties that are single level, and ones that won't have many repairs for the tenant to deal with. If you want to deal with an apartment, you will have to consider whether you want to rent to families, singles, or college kids to determine where you will purchase and how big each unit is.

Knowing what market you want to cater to can really help you think about the type of property you want to pick out. You never want to just pick the first property that comes up. It may require too much work, or it may not work for the kinds of renters in your area. Writing out this criteria ahead of time can help you prepare and will make it easier to find a property that will market itself to your target market.

Set up Your Plan and Pick Your Criteria

After you have spent some time looking at the market and learning everything you can about prices, rent averages, and what new things may come into the area, it is time to make out your personal plan and set your criteria. You should spend time writing out the plan and the goals so you can refer back to them and keep yourself on track when you start looking at properties.

When you are looking for a property and have decided that you can afford a home between $100,000 and $150,000, it can be easy to fall in love with a house that is $175,000; but that may be above your budget and you won't be able to afford it and make your mortgage payment. When you lay out your plans, you will do a better job holding yourself accountable through this process.

One thing that you may want to do before you even go and look at a property is to write out the criteria and take this paper with you. It is easy to see a property and think it is fine to change your rules or move a little bit off course. But soon, you get a lot of off courses and you get a property that is way too expensive, one that won't match with your current market, or one that will need too many fixes before you can even rent it out.

Arrange the Financing

Before you can put in an offer on a property, you need to figure out your financing. No seller will accept your offer if they don't have a pre-approval for the amount of the property. It can save a lot of time and will help you to know how much you can spend before you even take a look at the available properties for investing.

So, when you are ready to start looking for properties, make sure you talk about this with the bank. They will be able to give you an idea of how much you can buy and they can discuss the different financing options that you can use before you make your choice.

Remember, there are many places you can shop around with in order to find a good loan that will help you out. You need to find the right financial institution that will help you out. But they aren't just going to hand you the money and let you do what you want with it. They expect you to step forward and show that you are responsible, that you can handle the new business, and that you are not going to lose all their money.

This is why there are often some strict guidelines in place. You need a good credit score before you even start asking the bank to finance you. If you have any blemishes on the credit score, consider fixing those ahead of time so you can present a clean slate to the bank. You should have some kind of down payment since this is an investment rather than a personal property. Even some of the down payment can really help. And the bank will require that you have enough personal income to pay back the loan with your current income for that time when the loan is due before a tenant and in between tenants.

In addition to the things above, you need a few things. Some banks will require that you have a business plan to show how you plan to use the money, your expected timeline on the project, and when you plan to start earning money back. Take your time here because this really shows the bank how serious you are about this investment. A good business plan will make or break your bid for a loan.

You can consider looking at several different places to get your funding. Different banks can offer you different interest rates, different terms, and even different options when it comes to your loans. Even banks in the same area are going to show some differences. Shopping around a bit can help you get the best deal when it comes to your financing.

Begin Shopping Around for Some Properties

And now, the exciting part! You are going to start looking through your area to find a property that would be perfect as a rental property. You may have to take some time here and really search. But having patience will really pay off when you get into real estate because you will get the best deals.

You should start by looking on the MLS to see what properties are listed. This will provide you with the information you need on a lot of homes in your market. Even better, consider working with a real estate agent. They know the market and they can really help you through every step of the process. In this step, they are going to get you in touch with the information you need to really know which properties are best.

Make an Offer When You Find a Property

When you find the property and you have already checked it out, it is time to make an offer on the property. Your real estate agent, if you are working with one, is going to fill out the paperwork based on your request and then will submit that offer to your selling agent. Then the seller's agent will bring that offer to the seller and negotiations are going to begin from there.

You want to make sure that during negotiations, you only offer the amount that makes the most sense for you. You should offer less so that you have some room to negotiate with the seller. Before sending out an offer, be willing to walk away from the deal if it doesn't go the way that you want. This helps you to keep the emotions out and gives you the upper hand so you don't spend too much on the property.

During this time, remember that you are not only negotiating the price with the seller. Depending on how strong the deal is and how popular that property is, there are some other things you need to add into the offer for the seller to consider including:

- Inspection contingency
- Closing date
- Seller financial concessions
- Financing contingency

These are important items and can help you get things done and then walk away if there are more issues with the house than you knew about. Once you sign the agreement with the seller and all the terms are agreed upon, you can then move on to get the stuff done before your closing date.

Do Your Due Diligence

You and your seller have agreed on a price and the closing date is ready. Now you need to go through and do your due diligence. During this period, you need to spend the money on an inspector who can look over the property. They can let you know the condition of the house and if any of those defects are going to cost you money later on. If there is a major issue with the house, you have the option to go back and re-negotiate with the seller.

Now, you don't want to nickel and dime the seller if you are in a hot market. They can refuse to do the work and walk away from the deal. But it is fine to ask for some major problems with the home to be fixed. You can discuss things with your real estate agent to determine if the fix is something you should push for or not before purchasing.

This is also the time when you will finalize all the financial agreements with your lender. The title company will take over to help get the transaction taken care of and to ensure all the right papers get put in your day. When your closing date comes, you should sign documents before getting the keys to this property to take care of as your own.

Fix up the Property

In most instances, you should do some work to the property. The right price for a property is not going to show up unless you put in the work as well. Sometimes the work will be simple, like a new paint job and replacing a few appliances. Other times the property is going to need more work. Either way, you should have factored the cost for these improvements into your budget so there should be no surprises there.

As soon as you purchase the property, it is time to get the work done on it. You want to get the work started and completed as soon as possible. If it takes you six months to get the property ready for someone to live in, that means you have to come up with the mortgage payment for 6 months without any rental money coming in. Move quickly so that you can get your tenants in there and start earning money.

Find Your Tenants

After you find the property and you have fixed it up, it is time to find your tenants. You will never make any money on the property and will be responsible for the mortgage if you don't find any tenants to live in there. Some landlords start advertising the vacancy before the property is completely ready in the hopes of having someone ready to move in as soon as possible.

Tenants may be plentiful, but there are times when they will be hard to come by. It often depends on the area, the time of year, and more. Advertising early on can make it easier for you to find your target tenant as early as possible so you can start making money.

When you are looking for a tenant to live in your property, you should be very selective. A good tenant is going to stay in your property for a long time, providing you with a steady stream of income. You should have them fill out an application and provide a rental history and references to ensure that they will be reliable and won't cause more problems than it is worth.

Enjoy the Profits from Your Work

When you get to this point, congratulations! Your property is filled and you are going to earn money from your monthly rent. This may be a little bit slow in the beginning because you are paying off the mortgage and all the other expenses. But as you pay things off and potentially raise the rent as values appreciate in the future, you will start to earn more and more income. You can then decide whether you want to take on another rental property and grow your business and investment even more.

Chapter 8: I'm Low on Finances, How do I Get Started Quickly?

Some people worry about being able to start with a rental property. They are not able to come up with tens of thousands of dollars in order to put in a down payment, and they worry they will never be able to get into the market. The good news is that there are a few options that you can use in order to get into this market without having a lot of money. Some of the options that you have available when you are low on finances include:

Investing Without Using a Down Payment

When purchasing a property, it is sometimes hard to come up with a 20% or larger down payment. You may be low on funds, but still dream about investing in the real estate market. There are some options you can work with that will help you to invest, even if you only have a small down payment or no down payment at all.

First, you can consider working with seller financing. If you have a motivated seller, they may be willing to give you the loan for the property. You could offer to give them some higher monthly payments that can work as your down payment. You could negotiate a deal with the seller where they pay the down payment to the lender to help sell the property faster. They may expect you to pay them back, or they could do it as a way to lower the price for you. No matter which method you go with, you should write up an agreement with a real estate attorney to make sure you and the seller are protected from anything turning out badly in the agreement.

Another option is to lease the property with the option to buy later. You can slowly invest in the rental property by making payments on a lease agreement until you come up with enough money to buy. At least a few your payments would be credited to your purchase price. If you go with this option, make sure that the agreement states the final price rather than having it as an assumption. Define the exact amount of the rental payment that should go to the final purchase price so you are protected.

Working out a trade can be an option as well. This one is not as common since most buyers need to pay off the mortgage when they sell their house so they won't want to barter anything. But if you do this one, you would barter some other property you have or a specialized skill. You could offer furniture, artwork, appliances, and more to get the property.

And finally, you could decide to take over the mortgage payments for the other party. If you want to invest in some real estate but you aren't able to afford the down payment, you can offer to take on the mortgage payments in exchange for the deed. You need to look at the existing loan of the seller because some loans don't allow this kind of thing to happen.

There is a variation of this last one where you agree to take over some of the other debts of the seller such as their credit card payments, instead of doing a down payment. Put this all in writing because the seller may be nervous about doing this. You could easily not pay the amount on the credit cards and then the seller has the debt and a bad credit score with no way to get the house back.

Co-Investing with Someone Else for a Down Payment

Sometimes, you may need to work with someone else to get your properties. This can cut a bit into your profits, but when you share the work and share the expenses, it takes out some of the risks. The first thing you can do here is to bring in a partner. Both of you can pool together your money and then take on the expenses, the work, and the profits from that property. Make sure that the two of you write out a contract that is going to establish who is responsible for what, and how you plan to divide up the profits.

If you are stuck with who to invest with, consider doing it with a building contractor. This can be really helpful if you plan to do electrical, plumbing, and carpentry in the property and you don't have the right skills to do it on your own. Then you can take the profits that you make on that sale, share the agreed upon amount with the contractor and then save for your next property.

Borrowing Money to Get Your Down Payment

In some cases, you may decide that it is best to borrow money from friends or family. This is definitely a place where you are going to need to write out an official promissory note that has some due dates for the payments. You can include the interest rates that the other person will charge and whether or not they have any ownership in the property. You have to consider the relationship with the person you are asking money from. It is possible the rental property will be a failure and if you can't pay the money back like agreed, can this harm relationship? You have to consider whether the real estate venture is worth ruining your relationship with someone who is close to you.

You can also consider using a home equity loan to help you get started. We spent some time discussing this before, but this is an option for those who are low on start-up costs with your investment. These loans are not going to cost you any down payments and sometimes can offer you a lower interest rate than others.

This option is will allow you to take out a loan for the down payment on your project on top of the mortgage that you have on your personal residents. This is sometimes a second mortgage and other times it is a line of credit. You want to make sure that you can pay off this amount because you could risk losing your own home if you can't.

And finally, consider a microlender. These types of loans often go by the name of peer to peer lending and they will help a borrower find a relatively small loan. These loans are often going to be less than $35,000. You need to do some research on these and learn about the regulations and rules so you don't run into any misunderstandings about how they work later on in the process.

Chapter 9: Repairing and Maintaining Your Rental Properties

Once you have purchased your new property, it is time to get to work. There is likely to be a few things that you need to take care of in the property to make sure it is ready for the tenants to move into. If you did well with the seller, there shouldn't be anything major to work on at this point, so that is the good news here. But you are now in charge of this property. But once you buy a home or property, it is a continuous process of repair and maintenance. You have to clean up the property, conduct preventive maintenance, fix exterior and interior issues and damages, make sure all essential services are working (water, electricity, plumbing, heating, provided appliances and equipment), and ensure that everything works properly the whole time you own it—even if a tenant is living there.

The first thing is to do any renovations and updates. You may decide to add in a room, take down some walls to open it up, do some painting, do some landscaping, or anything else that you can to increase the value of the property. The more you can do for a low price, the better. This helps you attract more tenants and can allow you to ask for a higher rent.

In addition to these renovations to improve the value of the home, there are a few other things that you can do to help with routine property inspections and repairs of the property, whether you are preparing it before a tenant moves in or afterward:

- Keep the wood exterior on the home painted. This can lead to some softness and even deterioration of the wood if you don't keep up on this, and this repair can be really costly to work with.

- Check the dirt around your foundation. It should be sloping away from the foundation. If you see there are some holes around it, fill them and then add dirt backfill around it to help the water drain away, rather than inside and into the home.

- Check the gutters, especially in the fall. You want to keep these free of debris and leaves. Failing to do this can really let water back up into the gutters. The overflow from this could lead to water getting into the home and causing damage there. You can also add in some extenders to the downspouts so they are not able to empty to the foundation.

- Take some time to check the doors and windows for any gaps. Use some weatherproof sealant to help prevent water from getting into the home. These areas should be sealed up to make sure that water can't get in and cause damage. It is also a good way to keep the utility costs down because heat won't be able to get out.

- Take the time to inspect the trees on the property. Look for dead limbs or any that are hanging low and need some work. Look at the base of the tree. If you see that there is some rot on the bottom, they need to be cut down to avoid them falling onto your property.
- Check the roof occasionally. You want to see if there are any missing or damaged shingles. After some high winds or bad storms, be especially vigilant. These bad shingles can end up allowing water to get into the home, which can damage the property and cause mold to grow. Fixing these issues with drywall and mold cleaning can be very expensive,so stay on top of it before problems arise.

- If your property has a fireplace that burns wood, you should make sure that the chimney has an inspection and is cleaned out once a year. If you don't, it can cause a chimney fire. Make sure to give your tenants plenty of time to prepare for the cleaning to be done.

- To keep the property safe, you should clean out and inspect the heating and air conditioning systems at least one time a year. And each month, the filters should be changed. This ensures that the system will run in a more efficient manner and there won't be as much wear and tear.

- If your property does have a crawl space, then you or a professional needs to get into this area at least one time a year to check it out. Look along the plumbing and walls to see if there are signs of leaking. If you smell a musty smell, puddles on the floor of the crawl space, or water bills that are high, then there could be a problem. If you see that this area has some standing water, do not go in because illegal wiring could be there and you will get electrocuted. Call a professional contractor to help you get rid of that water and find out what is going on there.
- If your circuit interrupters have a problem, you need to test or trip them each month to make sure that they will function the way that you want. Failure to do this on a regular basis could result in the ground fault circuit interrupters that are not going to reset or not trip. You can either do this on your own or teach the tenants how to do it if they don't want you to come over all the time.

- Fix anything that goes wrong. Once the tenant moves into the home, you need to be prepared to take on the work if something stops working the proper way. Things are going to break or need to be fixed, and this becomes a bigger issue the longer you have the home. It is up to you to get it fixed, or hire someone else to fix it, within a reasonable amount of time after the tenant lets you know about it. If the issue at hand is going to cause harm and is an emergency to the tenant, you need to get over there to fix it right away.

In many cases, the tenant is going to be responsible for some things on the property, such as mowing and snow removal, unless this has been discussed ahead of time and is in the lease.

The tenant is also expected not to do any damage, beyond normal wear and tear, on the property.

If you fail to do the right maintenance or fix things when they break in the property, the tenant can withhold your rental payments and may be able to file charges against you. They have the right to void the lease and leave as well. If the tenant doesn't keep the home in good shape and pay their rent, you have some options in place as well.

Chapter 10: Tips for Working with Your Tenants

Once you have purchased a property to work with, you need to get tenants into the building. Without tenants, you will not earn any money and all the responsibility of paying for the mortgage and the other fees on the property will fall to you. The sooner you can get the tenant into the building and paying rent, the better off you will be in terms of getting a good return on your investment.

Getting tenants can be a challenge sometimes. You have to advertise for the tenant, and then when you get some interested parties, you have to do some screenings to ensure they are a good tenant and will stay with you while paying rent on time. It is important to take your time through this process because a bad tenant can be much worse than no tenant at all. Some of the steps that you need to do when selecting your own tenants include:

Advertising for Tenants

As soon as you own the property, consider listing it as a rental property. Going through all the steps that we will talk about in this chapter can take some time; and the earlier that you can get started, the earlier you can get that tenant in there and start making money. You can easily look through applications and do the screenings while you finish up any work on the property.

There are different methods that you can use to advertise your listing. You can start with your local newspaper. You can put a sign in front of the property to let those driving by know about the vacancy. You can use social media; make connections, use sites like Zillow, and more.

One of the best methods is with the word of mouth. You can enlist the help of your real estate agent and friends to help spread the word. This often works better than some of the other methods and can often provide you with better tenants than the other options as well.

Choosing the Best Tenants

As a landlord, you will quickly learn that there are good and bad tenants. While there is no screening method that will always guarantee you won't get a bad tenant–and many landlords who have been in the business a long time can tell you stories about that one bad tenant they will never forget–there are some factors that you need to pay attention to when you want to find a great tenant for the rental. Here are some of the things you should pay attention to when choosing a tenant.

Follow the Law
The first step here is to follow all the laws. A landlord must treat all of their prospective tenants in an equal manner. The Federal Fair Housing Act was put in place to help prevent landlords from discriminating against some tenants. You are not allowed to discriminate against a tenant because of a disability, their familial status, sex, religion, national origin, or race.

There are also many states that have some of their own Fair Housing Rules that you need to follow. Make sure that you check in on and adhere to any local laws that are in place as well.

Choose a Tenant That Has a Good Credit History

When picking out tenants, you want to make sure that you look for one who is financially responsible and is likely to pay their rent on time each month. There are two steps that you can do to help check the finances of the tenant and these include:

A. Verify the income.
   a. You want to find a tenant who makes at least three times the amount that you are charging in rent each month.
   b. Ask the tenant for copies of their pay stubs to prove income.
   c. Take the time to call the tenant's employer directly to verify information. You can ask about monthly earnings, attendance, how long the person was employed there, and to confirm that they are employed.

B. Run a credit check on them.
   a. This is going to show you if the tenant has a history of paying their bills on time.
   b. Check out the income to debt ratio the tenant has. They may make three times the rent; but if they have bills that eat up all that income, then you may not see the rent that much.
   c. See if the tenant has any bankruptcies, civil judgments, or prior evictions.

You may have to pay a bit to get these done, but they can reveal a lot of problems about a tenant that you won't be able to find out any other way. You should also write that you are going to verify information and do a credit check for all applicants on the applications. This can scare some of the bad tenants away and can save you a lot of time.

Do a Criminal Background Check

Criminal information about your potential tenants is a public record and you can see it at the courthouse in your area. You will be able to find out all the minor and major offenses of the tenant if any. You just need the name and date of birth for your tenant. Check on a valid ID to make sure the tenant is giving you the right information before you do this.

Before you do this, make sure that you understand the rules in your state. For example, in California, you are not able to discriminate against renters for certain criminal convictions. The type of crime is matter as well. A few speeding tickets are probably not enough to refuse someone unless there are other reasons along with this. But a tenant with a violent crime and drug conviction could be an issue and could be dangerous to the other tenants.

There also isn't a nationwide database of these criminal records so doing a thorough background check is hard and can take up a lot of time. Many landlords choose to have a professional company do the work for them to get this done without wasting their own time.

Look at the Past Rental History of the Tenant

If you can get this information, spend the time talking to a minimum of two of the tenant's previous landlords. This helps you to know whether the tenant is a problem. The more landlords you find on the list, though, the more likely that the tenant was an issue and you may not want to deal with them. Some questions that you can ask a previous landlord about a potential tenant include:

- Did the tenant spend a lot of time complaining? Did they cause a lot of problems with their neighbors?
- Did they cause a lot of damage to the apartment, besides the normal wear and tear?
- How well did the tenant keep the apartment and was it clean?
- Before they moved in, did the tenant give 30 days' notice? Why did the tenant move out? Did they break the rules or not pay their rent?
- Was the tenant known for paying their rent on time?

Now, there are times when the tenant may be a first-time renter, a recent graduate, or a student; it is possible that they don't have a rental history yet. You can still work with them. Just consider having them put a co-signer on the lease to protect you.

Choose Tenants Who Are Stable

When you look through the application of the potential tenant, look at their prior addresses and their history of employment. Do you notice that they move a lot or can't seem to keep a job? If you notice that the tenant moves often, this is something they will probably continue and it won't be long before you have a vacancy on your hands. If the tenant does not have a consistent employment history, they may find they are not able to afford the rent in a few months and you have to deal with an eviction.

Consider How Many Tenants for the Property

The more people you have in each apartment, the more noise, and more wear and tear that can happen to your investment. While there are no really specific rules for how many occupants can be in one room, under the Fair Housing Act, two people for each bedroom is usually reasonable. There are some exceptions to this including:

- State and local law: If your state or your local area has its own housing codes, you need to follow these.
- Size of the dwelling: A bedroom that is 500 sq. ft. can hold more people than a 250 sq. ft.room.
- A unit that has a den and a living room could hold more people than one that does not have.
- Age and number of children: It may be seen as discriminatory to refuse to rent out a one-bedroom house to two adults with an infant. But if you refuse to rent to two adults who have a teenager in one bedroom, that would be reasonable.

- You can choose a maximum number of people that are in an apartment, but you can't have a maximum number of children in the apartment.
- Limitations of the sewer and septic system: If the system capacity can only tolerate a certain amount of people, you can make some rules for this.

Go with Your Instincts

You can follow the screenings listed above, but you may find that your instincts are the best way to tell if the tenant is going to be a good one or not. If you spend some time talking to them and find that a tenant seems off or you do not feel comfortable with them for some reason, then trust these instincts. This may be the trick you need to avoid getting a bad tenant into your property.

Setting Up a Lease

Before the tenant can move into your property, make sure that you get them to sign a lease agreement with you. If a tenant is not willing to sign, this should send up some red flags and you may want to consider picking out someone else. A lease will protect both you and the tenant so not signing one is not in the best interests of either party.

The lease lays out everything that you and the tenant agree on. It will list the address of the property as well as contact information for you in case the tenant needs to get a hold of you. It states the monthly rent and when it is due, along with other charges if the tenant is late on their payments. It also lays out rent's validity period–allowing them to leave without penalties and giving you the freedom to change rent and terms when you want afterward–and it outlines the responsibilities of you as a landlord and of the tenant.

There are often templates that you can pick online to help you write out a good rental agreement. You can also work with a real estate lawyer to write one out. Make sure that all tenants will sign the agreement before you let them move in so that both parties know what to expect from each other and both parties can be protected.

Chapter 11: Exit Strategies When You Want to Move on

The goal of rental properties is to keep building your empire. You want to finish with the first property and then purchase another, and another, and another. Many people keep growing these until they can make a good passive full-time income, and then even hire a property manager who can do a lot of the work for them. But there are some situations where you may want to leave the rental investment. Some of these reasons include:

- You don't have a good experience with the process: Many people who exit their rental investment do it because they had a bad experience with a tenant. When you begin, realize that having a bad tenant is part of the process. You may just need to get a better screening process in place for your tenants so you make sure you don't have to go through that process again.

- You have some emergency: This could be a family or a medical emergency, a divorce, or something else that takes your attention away from your rental properties. If you just can't keep managing your rental properties, having that exit strategy can make it easier to move on.

- You find that you do not like to be a landlord or do not like to own these rental properties. You tried hard at this business, you analyzed and followed every step that is listed, but once you got into it, you found that you just didn't enjoy being a landlord. This can happen to anyone. There are two options here. You can use your exit strategy and get out of the market, or you can continue to grow your business and deal with the temporary dislike. Once the business has grown enough to support it, consider hiring a property management company to help take care of the work for you. Then you can let them be the landlord instead of doing the work yourself.

- You want to move to bigger and better investments: You may decide to get out of rental properties because you want to work on a different type of investment. If this is the reason that you want to exit the market, then you are heading in the right direction.

- The property you picked ends up costing too much and you don't earn a profit: This problem can occur if you aren't careful with the type of property you picked. Maybe you didn't do an inspection and the property had more work, or you may have thought that the property would earn more income than it does. In any case, you get started on this property and then find you can't make a profit. Even after getting past the first few months of paying off some of the repairs, the property still ends up sinking money and you can't get ahead. When the property is a big loss and you can't earn from it, then it may be the time to exit.

- You decide it is time to retire: After you have been in the rental property business for some time, you may decide that it is time to retire. Some people decide to hand this off to a property manager to ensure they can still earn an income. But others decide that when they retire, they do not want to deal with any of this anymore. If that is your choice, you may want to have an exit strategy to help you get out.

These are just some of the reasons why you may decide that exiting the property rental business is the right decision for you. Having an exit strategy in place from the beginning doesn't mean that you are hoping the project will fail. It simply means that you are preparing in case the investment isn't just right for you or if something else goes wrong.

Options for Your Exit Strategy

Basically, when you are ready to get out of the rental investment, you simply need to sell or otherwise get rid of the property that you own. There are a few different choices that you can go with when it is time to sell the property, but below are some of the most common options.

Sell It on MLS as Retail

The best option to go with to make the highest profit from the sale is to sell your property on MLS. You will need to pay some realtor commissions and deal with closing costs with this, but it can be worth your time.

The first step here is to find a qualified realtor to help you. It is preferable that your rental property is up-to-date and doesn't have any tenants living there at the time. This means that you may have some time when you won't get rental payments while you try to sell that property.

Normal homebuyers are looking for a nice house that is in a nice area. So when you purchase your property to start with, you need to keep in mind that you may try to sell it at some point and choose the area carefully. If your property is in the wrong area or you do not have enough time to fix it up, then it may be best to sell the property to an investor.

Sell It on MLS to Investors

If you find that the property is not going to work well when you try to sell it as retail, then you may want to still list it on MLS, but cater to investors. If you are doing the selling through MLS at all, then you should still use a realtor and look for one that has some experience working with other investors.

The best way to entice an investor is if the property currently has a tenant inside and the buyer will just be able to earn some cash flow from the moment they purchase it. You need to keep the property in good condition, though, and be honest with the buyer through the whole process. Remember what it was like when you became an investor? Your buyer is an investor here as well and they will want a good deal. This may help you sell the property faster, but remember that the investor will not want to pay the retail price, so you won't make as much with this option.

Do a For Sale By Owner (FSBO)

You also have the option to sell and market the property on your own. If you don't feel like using a realtor and spending money on them, you don't have to. You can always sell the property as a For Sale By Owner. There are a lot of options here, such as posting the property's information online or in the newspaper, or using word of mouth to get the information out.

Depending on the property and the situation around you selling the property, you may want to sell the house to traditional homebuyers or sell it to investors. Some sites that you can use to do a For Sale By Owner includeBiggerPockets Marketplace, Craigslist, and FSBO.

Sell with Owner Financing

Another tool that you have at your disposal is to sell the property through owner financing. You can market the property using some of the other options above, but then indicate that you also offer owner financing to the right buyer. You get the benefit of setting your own terms, which can open up the gates to other buyers who are less qualified. You may be able to find other investors this way or just open up the door to more potential buyers since you can get some who may not be able to purchase otherwise.

If you want to get out of the investment, but you don't need hard cash right now, this option would be a great one. You will still be holding the papers to the property during this time, but you still collect the cash flow. This basically makes you a note investor.

Sell the Property Back to the Turnkey Provider If You Bought It That Way

If you have purchased your property from a turnkey provider, then it is possible–in some cases–to sell that property back to the same provider. This is often best as a last option when the other ones are not working out and you really need to get rid of the property. The turnkey provider is not going to purchase the property from you without a huge discount, and you won't recover any of your money selling that way.

With this option, be prepared to lose money on the deal. The shorter the time frame that you hold onto the property, the more money you stand to lose with this one. Yes, purchasing from a turnkey is a good way to purchase a good rental property, but they can only offer these good deals if they have originally purchased them for an even lower price. Remember that when you consider this option.

When you get started with your rental property investments, you should have enough knowledge and preparation that the project will be successful. But sometimes, there are situations that go beyond our control and we decide that it is time to get out of the business. This chapter discussed some of the methods that you can use in order to get rid of the property and move on to other things.

Chapter 12: What If My Market is Expensive? How to Purchase Rentals in an Expensive Market?

Those who hope to invest in rental properties want to make a long-term passive income. While these rental properties can provide you with a great passive income if you do it right, investing in this manner can be risky. As the housing bubble shows, it is possible to lose a ton of equity in your property if you purchase at the wrong time.No matter what market you invest in, make sure that you start out the process by researching healthy prospects and establishing realistic rent prices and estimated profits.

There are times when the neighborhood you want to invest in will be more expensive. Some whole towns are expensive and you may have trouble even finding the first property you want to go with. Here are some tips that you can follow when you are ready to get into the real estate market with rental property investing:

Compare the Affordability of the Market

Currently, a lot of first-time homebuyers have trouble purchasing a property–which is why they rent–because some of the most affordable inventory is locked in negative equity. Almost 19% of homeowners right now are underwater on their mortgage, which means they wouldn't be able to sell off the property without having the cash to bring at closing. This low amount of inventory paired with some expensive rents means that most families are stuck renting without much of a chance to purchase a home.

This is a great market for landlords because you will be able to charge higher rates. But it also means that you have to deal with higher purchase prices in some popular areas as well. The median home value on the west coast can be high including Portland ($306,300), Los Angeles ($531,400), and San Francisco ($999,400). These numbers can be seen in other parts of the country as well. A landlord may be able to charge more in rent, but they need significant capital to get into the market and compete with other investors if a reasonable property becomes available.

The good news is that these same kinds of areas are the same ones that renters are willing to pay for. The average rent in Portland, for example, is $1,521 a month, and those in Seattle will pay more than $2,000 on average. If can purchase a property in these areas or others, you will be able to charge a lot more in rent payments each month and make a lot more profit in the process as well.

Seek out Moderate Pricing

In these expensive areas, a rental property buyer needs to invest a lot of money upfront. Your hopes here are the appreciation of the property over time and you will start to see some positive cash flow from rent. Though some of these places are expensive, the appreciation is still likely there, which means that a long-term investment here will be important for gaining profits. You can consider your realistic returns by subtracting operating costs from the rent income, and then minus the amount you have to pay each month on the mortgage.

Here is a relevant example: A regular mortgage on a property is $500,000 and you put 50% down. The loan has a 4% interest rate, so you will end up paying $2,000 a month, including insurance and property taxes. Imagine this is a property that has 10 units and you could earn $3,500 every month. After you add in your operating expenses at 35%, or $1,225 each month, that gives you a yield of $2,275. Then take the mortgage payment and the owner yields $275 a month. You have to determine if that is enough to make it worth your time.

The more you can invest of your own each month, the lower your mortgage and the higher the monthly returns. Without capital to help you purchase these rentals with cash—which is something that can easily happen in this higher priced areas—you will need to wait to make a purchase or find lower-priced buildings. Make sure you stay away from prize properties because they won't make you any money and they aim for working-class neighborhoods that will charge moderate rents.

Even in these higher-priced areas, you will be able to find a property that meets your needs. It may just take more initial investment and you may have to wait around a bit longer to find the property. You may also need to do some more work on a few properties to get the price reduced to a more affordable level.

Budget in the Operation Expenses

Before you decide to purchase any rental properties, especially in an expensive area, you need to take the time to plan out your property management strategy. Some owners like to run the whole thing on their own, from signing a lease to working with the tenant and handling any emergencies.

This method can work to help cut out some of your costs. However, it may not be the right approach for you especially if you don't know how to do a lot of the handyman options. If on-call management is not best for you, then you can start to look for some property management companies who can help you out. Just make sure that you take the time to find a good one, and add this into your budget for the rental property.

Start Your Search as Early as Possible

If you are serious about this new investment, you should start your rental property search as early as possible. In fact, you may want to start this at least three to six months before you are ready to purchase. This may seem like a long time to do your search, but it holds a few advantages to the investor over some other options.

First, it allows you as the investor to really research the market around you and gain a good familiarization of the current values of properties near you. If you jump right into the market and plan to make a purchase in just a few days, then it is hard to know whether you are getting a good deal on a property or not.

If you are searching online for your rental property, don't just rely on the pictures that you see when making a purchase. Go and visit the units and examine some of the comparable sales. You want to walk through each of these properties, especially if you plan to charge enough to reach market rents.

Work with an Agent

For those who want to purchase rental properties in a more expensive area, you may want to consider working with a buyer's agent. These agents won't cost you anything–the seller takes care of all real estate agent's commissions–and they can provide you with a lot of resources. They know the best areas of the town, they can give you hints on cheaper units coming up, and they can handle all the paperwork when the process is underway. Since they don't cost you anything and they provide you with a lot of great resources, it is worth your time to use these individuals when looking for a property.

Consider Whether It Is a Good Idea to Live Onsite

One way to select your investment properties is to look for any characteristics that you would want in your own home. Often, the same amenities that appeal to you can also be appealing to your renters. You can look for things such as simple commutes, grocery stores and other shops nearby, and being close to the local areas.

If you purchase a property that you love and would like to live in, it will be more likely to be maintained by the renters as well, and they will also show the right commitment up to keeping this investment.

You can also choose to actually live in the property. If you are just moving to a new area, or if you want to save some of your living costs when you get started with this investment, then consider moving in to one of the properties. Onsite homeowners know about living in those properties and this makes it easier for them to respond to tenants and fix anything that comes up. Buyers who live onsite can get better financing options on the mortgage and can get others to pay for their own living costs, saving some money in these more expensive areas.

Purchase a Property That Is Already in Good Condition

You may be able to get a property for a good price, but if it will require too much work, you did not get a good deal. You will be required to fix up the property ahead of time, or no tenants will come and live there so you won't make any profits from rent. You want to purchase the property in the best possible conditions that you can.

One thing that you can do here is to invest in an inspection of the property before you close on the home. If the property requires some upgrades—whether you noticed those or they showed up in the inspection—the buyer needs to estimate how much it will cost to do these improvements and if they are affordable before they purchase the property.

If the inspection shows up any issues, you have the options to either walk away from the deal at that point or you can also negotiate some credits from a seller or require that they fix the issue before you purchase. Once it is a done deal, the owner should quickly complete the rest of the upgrades to ensure that the property is safe and ready for tenants to move into.

You should purchase a property that needs a little work. That is the best way to get a good deal on the property and actually make some profits. But if you have to put so much into it that your profits disappear, you are going to be disappointed in the results.

Really Watch the Costs and Potential Profit

When you purchase these rental properties in an expensive area, you should be careful and really review how profitable the operation will be. Figure out what the unit seller is charging for rent. Figure out how much it will cost to do taxes, insurance, and repair of the property. You should also look at how often tenant turnover occurs and whether the property is already cash flow-positive or if you are going to have to work to improve this. You can check for any property disclosures that show some damages or if there are signs for repairs in the future that can be costly.

You need to go through all these costs and determine if they are the right options for you. You need to walk away from a property because it is not going to actually make you a profit. If the taxes, insurance, upgrades, and mortgage will be higher than what you can reasonably expect to get for monthly rental payments, then it doesn't matter how good of a deal it is. You should not purchase it.

Rental properties can be difficult,to begin with, but when you are in an expensive market, your costs to start will be higher. You can still make a good profit in the process, but you may need to take a bit more time to put together a down payment and you have to work smarter in the market. But, with some good planning and some patience, you can still make money in an expensive market.

Chapter 13: How Do I Build a Rental Property Empire

Once you have purchased your first property and it seems to be doing well with some positive cash flow from rent, you may want to figure out how you can expand this and make an empire. Over time, you may be able to purchase one property right after another. Each of these can provide you with a positive cash flow that you can use to purchase more properties, or even to help you earn an income. If you are successful, and you purchase enough properties that do well, you can hire a property manager to handle the rentals for you while you earn a full-time passive income and get to accomplish a greater of amount what you want.

The next step here is to come up with a plan and some goals that will help you to build up your rental property empire. Plans and goals are going to work the best when you add specifics and details. If you say that you want to be successful, you have to figure out what that means. Each person defines success in a different manner, some will see it as earning a lot of money, and others are happy if they own a house. The more specific you can make the plans for building your own rental property empire, the easier it will be for you to put those into action.

Below are some of the basics that you can include in your plan when you want to build up a rental property empire.

- How much money do you think the property will generate?
- How much money is needed to start?
- What financing option do you plan to use?
- What type of property will you purchase each time?
- When do you want to purchase the first property, the second property, and so on?

In order to answer these questions, you must take the time to research the market you are going to invest in. If you jump into this option without knowing much about the market, you are not going to see much success with the process. Once you answer the questions above, you will then need to expand out your plan to include things like:

- How will you find a property to purchase?
- How do you plan on managing the property?
- How do you plan to repair that property?
- Do you have any plans for saving money if you need to?

You should write out this plan for each property that you want to purchase. To really help yourself build up a great rental property empire, you need quite a few properties. Then, as you receive rental payments each month, you will be able to earn cash flow from that, while also paying off the loan with each property. Over time, as you pay off everything, you earn more and more profits in the process.

You must start out with your first property. This guidebook has concentrated most of its time on getting you that first rental property. That first property is usually the hardest one to get. You don't know how to work on the market and you should take your time to find it rather than rushing in. That first property is basically a trial run, a learning experience. You will make a lot of mistakes, but you will also learn a lot on the way so that you do better the next time around.

After you have gotten the first property up and running and you have the hang of how things work, you can then start working on the second property. You have a few options here. First, you can save up a bit of your profits each month to help you get enough for a down payment on the second property. Or, you can use the equity you earn in the first property–this property earned equity because of the mortgage payments you make, using your rental properties–to help secure a loan.

This is where a good loan officer can possibly help you out. They can explore different options with you to get you the best rates and options when it is time to work with a second property. You will then follow the same steps again: looking for a good property, making an offer, fixing it all up, and then finding the right tenants. You can then manage that property, get it all set up and making a profit before moving on to your third, fourth, fifth, and more properties.

The more properties you own, the faster your empire is going to grow. This may require some investment, and can even take many years depending on how well you can find properties and earn a profit. But over five or six years, you can start to get a few properties and start that empire. Each property is going to earn you more equity and more profits, which makes it easier to purchase the next property. That first one is always the hardest because you have nothing, but as you move through this process, things get easier.

Over time, you may have enough properties to make a passive income and can leave your regular job to take this on full-time. Even better, you may have enough properties that you can hire a property management company to handle the day-to-day operations, while you take the rental payments as a passive income and just enjoy life. And that is the ultimate goal with your empire: to turn this into a passive income so you can make as much as you want while someone else takes care of it all.

It may be a rough start with the first property, but no matter how hard it is, just keep going since you are still learning. Each property that you pursue after this will be easier to handle, and you will find that this is a very profitable way to make money.

Chapter 14: Tips to Help Every Beginner Get Started and See Success with Their Investment

As a beginner, you are probably excited to get out there and purchase your first property. You have big dreams of getting that property, finding your first tenants, and earning a check. But there is a lot of work that goes into one of these investments and you want to make sure that you are doing it the right way. Here are some of the best tips that you can follow as a beginner to ensure you can see this rental property investment become as profitable as possible.

Always Have Reasonable Expectations

You may have heard the stories of someone who got into rental property investing and then a year later, they were making $400,000 a year while vacationing. This is not a reasonable expectation to have. Over time, as you purchase more properties and your rents increase, you may be able to do this with the help of a property manager. But you cannot go from nothing to high wages in just a few months. And if someone tells you that you can, then you should run the other way from that scam.

While it is a good idea to have the goal of a positive cash flow, you should never expect that after a year in the market you can already live the high life. For the first few years at least, these rental properties are probably going to be part-time and side incomes that you can use to help build your empire. You won't be able to make the big money until much later on. Be sure to keep all your expectations in check so that you make reasonable decisions about your properties and can actually earn an income.

Do the Research About the Market Ahead of Time

You should never just get into this type of investment without doing some research. Many investors are reckless having known that there can be a passive income in rental properties. So they will go and find their first property without knowing what the market prices are, how much they will have to spend to fix it up, or how much they can charge in rent. They easily spend too much and they have to fix too much on the property. The rental payments may not be enough to cover the costs they incur.

It is always important to take the time to learn about the market and everything that you need to do to make rental properties as profitable as possible. You can benefit from watching the market for two or three months before even looking at loans or looking for a specific property to purchase. This helps you to know the market and what you can reasonably expect when you get into it. Those who don't rush into this investment are the ones who have the most luck and see results with their rental property empire.

Always Inspect the Property

An inspection can make a big difference on whether or not you purchase the property. You can do an inspection and get a good idea on whether the property is actually worth the money you are going to spend or not. If you find a major issue in the property, you still have time to back out without spending anything. Or, to help you get the property without spending as much money, you can ask the seller to shoulder the repair cost or just deduct whatever cost that will incur from what you owe to the seller.

Even if the inspection doesn't find anything major that you need to fix or be concerned about, you can still use it as a way to help you determine what needs to be done to make the home more presentable. You can work with a general contractor to see what things will cost, such as adding in an extra bedroom or fixing the plumbing, so you can add this into your costs when determining the profitability of the property.

Find a Good Balance Between Your Earnings and the Effort You Put in

When you get started with this kind of investment, you need to figure out how much work you want to put in. Do you plan to work with a property management firm or do the work yourself? This will matter because it can take up either more of your time or more of your potential profits. Not being careful with either one can be a hassle.

Some landlords decide that they want to take on all the work of the property and be more hands-on. That allows them to keep more of their profits in their own pockets. But taking care of even one property–much less multiple units at once–can get really time-consuming to work on. If you have another job, kids, a family, and other obligations, you may find that all of your free time is taken up with the properties.

If you don't have the time and energy to be a hands-on landlord, you will want to hire a property management team. This helps you to still make an income, but not have to spend your whole life at the property. While it is fine to do some of the work on your own to save money, you don't want to end up spending all day at the property only to make a few hundred dollars each month.

Know All the Rules in Your Area (Both Federal and State Laws)

Depending on where you live, there will be different federal and state laws that will say what you are responsible for and what you are liable for as a landlord. Before you sign a lease with any tenant, you are expected to know all of these laws. You cannot claim ignorance when something happens.

You need to spend time reading up on the laws and regulations for landlords in your area to make sure that you don't miss out on anything. You can also check up on the responsibilities for the tenants as well to make sure that you understand what your job is and what needs to be done by the tenant. This can take some time, but it is much better to do this now rather than having to spend time in court later because you missed out on something. If you are uncertain about a rule or something similar, then you should consider seeking legal counsel to help keep you safe.

Check That Your Leases Are Legal

You need to be extremely careful about the kind of lease that you are writing up for your tenants. There are certain legal terms allowed and certain ones that should be avoided to ensure that your lease is legal and that you are protected if it is time to evict the tenant from the property. If you make a mistake on the lease, then it is very difficult to litigate when the tenant violates the terms, even if you verbally agreed to certain things.

You should consider hiring an attorney to help you out. They can draw up a lease that is legal and will protect you and the tenant according to the laws in your local area. You can use this lease for all of your tenants and it can be used to protect you when things go wrong with them. You can ask the lawyer to help you write out the terms and the lease in a way that you can add in the names, dates, rent, and other details about the agreement so it is unique for each tenant.

Work with a Real Estate Agent

We have mentioned this a few times in this guidebook, but when you are looking for the perfect rental property, you should consider hiring a real estate agent to help you get your first property. You could try to do the work on your own, but since a real estate agent doesn't charge you for their services as the buyer, it is often better to work with one to get the job done.

Your real estate agent can work with you from the moment you start looking until you close on the property. They can help you find some of the best investment properties because they have more networks and connections than you might have. Then, when you are ready to purchase the property, they can do the paperwork, help you with negotiations, and put the right contingencies into place so you can walk away from the deal if things go wrong. Your agent can help with inspections, any renegotiations, and everything else until you close on the property and have the keys in your hand.

Getting started in rental properties is a great way to put your money to work for you. It takes some investment and risks in the beginning. But, over time, you are going to earn a steady paycheck each month, especially if you get that investment to grow into more than one property and provide you with a growth in equity as well. There is no investment quite like rental property investing, and these tips will give you a chance to get ahead in the market!

Conclusion

Thank you for making it through to the end of *Rental Property Investing*. Let's hope it was informative and able to provide you with all of the tools you need to achieve your goals whatever they may be.

Once you have made up your mind in what you are looking for in a property, the next step is to get into the rental property investing business. This is an exciting way to help you earn money on the side, or even as a full-time income, without entering the stock market or worrying about any of the things that happen in that investment. Rental properties can benefit you in so many ways. They help you to earn an income and to earn equity and you have the option to sell the property when you are done at a higher price–thanks to the rise in property values–so you can make even more money in the process.

This guidebook took some time to discuss rental property investing and all the steps that you need to follow to get started with this type of investment. Starting out in this kind of investment, though, is a long journey before you become a successful rental property investor. It also takes some money to get started with and there are some risks. But if you really do your research and put in the time and effort to find a good property, this can be a great way to make some money in this type of investment.

When you are looking at some of your options for investing and you are not sure where to begin, make sure to check out this guidebook and learn more about rental property investing today.

Finally, if you find this book useful in any way, a review on Amazon is always appreciated!